APR   1995

OUT OF THE
MADNESS

OUT OF THE MADNESS

MADNESS

FROM THE PROJECTS TO A LIFE OF HOPE

JERROLD LADD

WARNER BOOKS

A Time Warner Company

Copyright © 1994 by Jerrold Ladd
All rights reserved.

Warner Books, Inc., 1271 Avenue of the Americas, New York, NY 10020

W A Time Warner Company

Printed in the United States of America
First Printing: July 1994
10 9 8 7 6 5 4 3 2 1

Library of Congress Cataloging-in-Publication Data
Ladd, Jerrold.
    Out of the madness : from the projects to a life of hope / by
Jerrold Ladd.
        p.   cm.
    ISBN 0-446-51744-5
    1. Ladd, Jerrold.   2. Afro-Americans—Texas—Dallas—Biography.
3. Journalists—Texas—Dallas—Biography.   4. Afro-American
journalists—Texas—Dallas—Biography.   5. Dallas (Tex.)—Biography.
I. Title.
F394.D219N45   1994
976.4'281100496073'092—dc20
[B]   93-41118
                                                                    CIP

Book design by Giorgetta Bell McRee

This book is dedicated to every black who would rather be burned at the stake than die with no honor.

"Be not conformed to the ways of this world but be ye transformed by the renewing of your mind."
—Romans 12:2

CONTENTS

CONTENTS

INTRODUCTION

by Mark Mathabane

Black parents rose in the morning and turned into the living dead," writes Jerrold Ladd in his searing autobiography chronicling the nightmares and horrors he witnessed and experienced coming of age in the drug-infested, poverty-stricken and violent ghettos of Dallas.

Raised by an abusive and drug-addicted mother, whose own mother had abused her and died from a drug overdose, Jerrold, a precocious and sensitive child, soaked in all the phantasmagoric goings-on of that netherworld of lost souls in which violence, casual sex, poverty and drugs were a daily fixture.

At seven he witnessed two bigoted white policemen almost let his mother be killed by drug dealers she had crossed. While still a child he suffered the ultimate man-child trauma when his mother's philandering and drug habit drove his father to abandon them. And before Jerrold reached his teens he had seen friends murdered or transformed into dope fiends, thieves and prostitutes, by poverty, parental neglect, broken homes, lack of opportunity and racism.

Remarkably, Jerrold not only survived, he did so with his intellect and soul intact. His experiences and enormous talent have made him one of the most powerful young black writers to emerge on the contemporary literary scene and to give impassioned utterance to the voiceless and disenfranchised millions who daily languish and die in the Sowetos and Beiruts of America.

Jerrold's story speaks for and to a generation. He tells us, in riveting and poignant details, without self-pity and with eloquent rage, about his complicated relationships with "Momma," his strong-hearted but naive older sister Sherrie, and his quiet, children-loving brother Junior. He introduces us to a motley of unforgettable characters who peopled the projects of Dallas: Ugly Biggun, the bully; his mother's string of lovers; grandmotherly Ruthy Mae, "who gave like Jesus"; the "Afro bandits," who executed people in the drug trade; and the many hardworking men and women who miraculously found ways to survive in the raging hell which daily twisted the humanity of countless of their brethren into something almost bestial.

Through Jerrold's eyes we feel the degradation suffered by blacks quarantined in America's ghettos, and the desperation with which they often seek solace and meaning for their hopeless lives in religion, alcohol, casual sex and drugs. We grieve with him at the sheer waste of young black lives deprived of hope, guidance and support. And lastly, we rejoice and marvel when he miraculously makes it *Out of the Madness*.

Jerrold escaped by embracing Malcolm X's credo of self-reliance, and by realizing early that knowledge was power and the key to liberation. He became a voracious reader. He discovered his African heritage, with which he forged a new identity. "Knowing the great accomplishments of my people, when they existed in their own civilizations, started a chain reaction that would change the foundation of my mind."

He also benefited from rare friendships with whites who helped him along and gave him important breaks. He learned from his mistakes, fought for the right to be a father to his out-of-wedlock daughter, and strove to help his mother kick the drug habit. By accepting responsibility for his own life and destiny, even when racism was a daily and deadly reality, Jerrold understood the most important lesson of survival.

Out of the Madness provides disturbing similarities between apartheid South Africa and America. In both societies the majority of blacks fight for survival in violent worlds which breed the same frustrations, desperation, rage, bitterness, violence and self-destruction. The men are often emasculated by the system, and many in turn abuse their women, neglect their children, and even kill each other. In the mean streets of South Africa and America innocence dies young; children cannot afford to be children and live; and few survive long enough to understand what it truly means to be a human being.

Jerrold Ladd survived the madness. The scars his soul bears have enabled him to pen a deeply felt and beautifully realized memoir of what it means to be a young black male in America's equivalent of the Alexandras and Sowetos of apartheid South Africa. It is a story of survival with dignity and pride against insuperable odds. So universal is its message, and so sincere its anguished voice, that it emphatically makes its appeal to the human heart by which we all feel, and the conscience by which we seek to do right.

1

WELCOME

My body felt hotter than the sun scorch coming through my bedroom window. My mother had just told me my fever was 103, though she didn't need to. Slowly I turned onto my side and laid my scrawny arm on the sill. When I touched the metal trimming, heat shot through my arm. I jerked away and saw the skin already blistering on my forearm. In the delirium of fever, I had forgotten just how hot that window could become.

This was west Dallas housing project heat. Just like the life here, it was thick, foul, and hard to breathe. Today, a morning in July 1977, the heat hovered over my bed like a vulture surveying its prey. Today, it was unbearable.

Normally, I could have withstood the heat, even the fever. They were not uncommon. But an unusual anger was sapping my strength, an anger I couldn't release. Two white police officers had almost let my mother die the previous evening.

Yesterday, I heard voices coming from the living room that did not belong in our house. I peeked around the corner of the stairs and saw two men holding revolvers against the heads of my mother and stepfather, hollering about how tough they were. My parents had swindled drug money from them. One of the men looked at me. I dashed past him, running through the back door of our apartment as fast as I could to where my brother and sister were playing.

Sherrie, my older sister, made me run across the wide field to get the cops assigned to the fire station. I ran like a deer, death, blood, and murder running through my head, my lungs screaming for air. I hoped that since the men had noticed me, maybe they would spare my parents. Many parents had been shot in the head lately.

When I arrived at the firehouse, I told the Dallas police officers that men were in my house with guns and were about to kill my parents. They took one look at me, this little black scrawny kid, then casually continued discussing a hunting trip. They took their unconcerned time, no hurry, no rush.

If I had not been seven, bony to the bone from starvation, and in such confusion, I would have hit those white cops, pounded them with my seven-year-old's fury. The nerve! After I had sought help from the only other adults a kid is supposed to trust besides his parents. The nerve! After I had told them that men were in my house with guns and were about to kill my mother. The nerve! To make me race against time for my mother's life, the most important person in the world to me, then be shown that it doesn't count, that it isn't more valuable than a lousy conversation.

When the cops and I finally returned fifteen minutes later, I looked inside before entering. There was no blood on the floor, no dead bodies lying around. The men had left. My mother wasn't concerned at all. She told the cops everything was okay.

The following morning I was still upset over what had happened as I lay on my used flea-populated mattress. It stank from the piss of other children, and was becoming soaked from my sickly sweat—mostly because there were no sheets. It was too hot, anyway, for sheets.

The project heat. It was worse than the dirty clothes scattered around my room, worse than the mildew, the crusty white walls, and the spiders, roaches, and other bugs that lived in the apartment.

I decided to get out of bed. I knew the best way to fight the fever, the heat vulture, and the anger was to get up, walk on the hard quarry tile, which looked like a warehouse bathroom floor, and find some food. Before I could, though, my mother entered the room with two pieces of chicken. My appetite left.

"Here, Jerrold, you want some chicken?" she asked while looking at her frail son, her youngest of three. But I just sat there, shadowed by my woolly hair, looking with my big rabbit eyes, which missed nothing, examining my mother's face. For the second time in an hour she had spoiled my appetite.

"Are you still feeling bad?"

"Yes, ma'am," I said.

"Momma is going to go and get you something for that fever. Okay?"

"Yes, ma'am."

She, twenty-seven, thick long hair, baby smooth skin, attractive, sat the chicken down and left the room again. My appetite came back. In a few minutes I had devoured the bird pieces, using my fury for strength. But I was still angry at her for almost getting herself murdered. It was her fault. She should not have run away with that man's money, the person who had sent the hitmen to frighten her. Thank God that visit had been only a warning.

But I knew she would continue to do wrong, for she was compelled by a force more powerful than love, hate, hunger, or death. More important than her children, her dignity, herself.

She would do it again, and again, until she was forever damaged or killed. As a teenager, I would hear the story from her, how her mother started her on dope.

Before moving to the west Dallas housing projects, she had lived with her mother and seven brothers and sisters in a weathered shack in west Dallas, around 1957. As the oldest of eight, she had little time for anything but cleaning, cooking, and washing and no time for games and other things young girls love to do. Although she wanted to go to school, her mother made her drop out at age fourteen. After all, that's what kids were for, she would show. Not to love, nourish, teach, or help plan for life, but to clean, cook, and wash. But my mother had a plan to get away from her mother, who ran a slave camp, who stayed high off prescription medication, and who was concerned mainly with men and not her children: Marry young.

When her young mind was closing on that answer, my future mother became pregnant with my sister, Sherrie. She was fifteen. The baby's father didn't marry her. With a young child of her own, she couldn't stick around a house with seven yelling, screaming, starving, desperate brothers and sisters in a swamp of poverty. And she had no need for a sinister mother who would find a way to use her for her welfare checks. So she met and married Paul Ladd. Then, sometime during the early years of their marriage, my brother, Junior, and I were born.

I still longed for my father. I missed how he used to wrestle and put us on his tall shoulders, and missed how he would throw big sticks into pecan trees and make us scramble at his feet, seeing who could pick up the most pecans. I missed the cool house my father provided, where my brother and I would take the phone receivers and use them for walkie-talkies. And I missed our clubhouse, which my sister and we boys spent days fixing up.

But these good times were a thing of the past, had ended when my grandmother started my mother. It happened in a bathroom in one of the many shabby apartments we moved to, when one of her many migraines was at full blast.

"I know what you can take for that headache," her mother had said. She handed my mother a syringe and a heroin pill. Then, with the coaxing and reassurance that only a mother can give, she showed my mother how to work the drug into a batter and inject it into her arm. She handed down the force that had made her neglect her own children and many others neglect their children. It was the same force that would make my mother neglect us. She also handed down the force that destroyed herself. In 1979 she died from a drug overdose.

After my mother became addicted, failure came fast within her marriage. She misused her minimum-wage-earning husband. She broke him. She sold their appliances. She ran off with men who supplied her dope. She left us, her children, naked and freezing on cold winter streets. Neighbors would keep us until our thoughtful dad, who cleaned, cooked, and washed, came home. One night they had argued.

He left her that day, after they had a big fight in the living room because she had left earlier without letting my dad know where she was going. Usually a quiet man, he shouted and called her names, believing she was returning from a boyfriend's house. In response, my mother hit him in the face several times, while doing her share of name calling. Fed up, my dad told her to get out and to take her kids with her. That's when my eyes lit up! I grabbed his leg and hung on; my brother joined me.

"Go on, son, go on with your momma," he kept saying.

"No, Daddy, we want to stay here with you."

I remember screaming and kicking as she dragged me away from my father. I knew things were going to be dreadful without him. Soon, he would have nothing to do with us. The next morning we had moved in with a lady in the projects. Weeks later we had our own project unit.

* * *

The small ants, unlike the monster red ants usually rampant around the projects, had started a new trail from under my bed, where I still lay. It led to the meatless chicken bone on the side of my bed. The ants scampered about, scavenging for meat particles. Another trail led to my closet, where bundles of old clothes, which had not been washed for months, were oozing foul vapors. That was my wardrobe. Up my windowsill, past the scorch, and down the outside bricks, the two ant trails merged and disappeared in the brown grass of the front yard.

Moments later, my mother returned to my room with two Anacin, something she could get even when she couldn't get food. I took the pills while she watched. My throat was raw. She wasn't high, as I clearly saw by her alert eyes, but give things a few hours, a couple of minutes. She never stayed down too long. As always, she wasn't able to hide her unhappiness, even while standing there. Sometimes she tried, offered a smile, a kind word, some pocket change for candy. But most of the time she stayed angry.

It was not a mean anger, but a desperate one—especially when she had a hard time getting another dose. Shout, whoop, beat, the rage of the devil would come from her. What could I do? I was a scrawny kid who was so loyal to his mother that I would have walked the earth barefoot for the Anacin she was addicted to or the cigarettes she demanded I borrow from strangers when she was high. What could I do but be loyal to her?

Uneducated, unschooled to the streets, and vulnerable, she was easy prey for people who would take advantage of her. With three children, my mother had been placed inside the projects by the federal housing people. With her new heroin habit, no family support, and no husband, she slipped and began to crumble. She worried, cried, beat us, and dreamed in her heroin high. Her face became a picture of worry.

What could she do with no knowledge, no skills, no ambition, and little support? And living in a place not unlike Hitler's concentration camps? So she worried, worried about getting the next heroin pill, which never failed to make the unyielding hardness of her life go away.

My rage at the cops had really left with the eating of the chicken, so I went into the sparsely furnished living room, which had one couch and a picture on the wall of some dogs playing cards. Junior had spread cards in strategic positions around the living room, playing a game we called Army Man. Though muscular and strong, he was very gentle. That was his manner, caring and affectionate. He was nine, with a narrow head and scalp-short hair. He had become quiet and despondent once we entered the projects.

But Junior loved kids and kids loved him. He would push them around all day in a shopping basket from the Tom Thumb grocery. To protect them from the scorch, he would cover the basket with an old blanket held up by a stick. The kids would laugh and pretend they were on long journeys as my brother maneuvered the basket down twisted sidewalk paths, under bare trees, and along glass-littered street curbs. He and the children would play all day, until the fear of deeds done in the dark sent them hurrying home. He was remaining gentle, regardless of what my mother was doing.

My sister, Sherrie, who was the oldest, had probably left to get away from my mother and the house. She was being made into a young mother—cleaning, mending, and scrubbing, though hardly any cooking took place—when she should have been studying, maturing, preparing for life. Sherrie was very fair-complexioned, yellow, some would say, short and shapely. Her intelligence was average, her loyalty to our mother vigorous. She was even more naive than our mother about the streets but was strong-hearted and had a solid will. Trying to hustle up money, school supplies, clothes, and food kept her busy.

Past the cracked wood of the front door, the torn screen, and the porch, another ant trail, made from the muscle red kind, etched its way toward the nearby ant bed on the side of our project unit. I followed the trail of the single-minded worker ants, who were uncompromising in their drive to beat winter, to beat the insanity of failure. I sat barefoot on a lime-green pickle bucket some kid had left near the ant bed.

Like the ants, the project units were in the thousands, on the west side of the Trinity River. The Trinity River, as distinct as the former Berlin Wall, was a clear boundary between the projects and north Dallas, the white side of town. Several simple bridges allowed travel over it. Within the Trinity, marsh and grass hid stolen cars, snakes, and dumped bodies. The river smelled rotten; and the smell often drifted into the projects, settling on the buildings.

The vast projects were divided into three groups: Elmer Scott, George Loving, and Edgar Wards, with a network of trails connecting them. Eight apartments were carved from each unit and numbered like jail cells. Made of bricks, they looked as if someone took a few old dirty chimneys, molded them together, and cut out windows. Clotheslines crossed in the backyards. Inside, roaches and rats roamed throughout the night, in our iceboxes, closets, and beds. Spiders and their webs were in every corner. The toilets always flooded; we sometimes relieved ourselves outside on the ground. Hot water was rare. Didn't matter to me: I never took baths anyway.

There was heat, but no air-conditioning. Some families had fans that they placed in wide-open windows to bring in the cooler air, when it was cooler. Others had old-fashioned blow fans that stored insulated water in small water tanks. But most families, like mine, had nothing. On long hot Texas nights, Junior and I usually tossed, turned, and sweated, unless a cool late night breeze brought us temporary relief. We would lie awake sometimes, waiting on that breeze. But when it passed us by, we would toss and sweat all night. Then the heat would wake us early in the morning.

Noise echoed throughout the units day and night, with every-

one sitting on his or her porch when the apartments became
unbearably hot. Radios would blare music, mostly blues and
mellow jazz. Crowds of young, lusty boys and teenage girls with
their babies would gather on the corners, on porches and in
parked cars. But not too close to the dope dealers.

Since there were few streetlights that worked, the dark darkness gave the place an eerie, wasted look. Teenage boys roamed
though the three sections late at night, to visit girls or the
marijuana house in George Loving. Fights, rapes, and arguments
were as common as the fear and grief that gripped this place.

Set up near the projects, across the wide fields, were rowdy
gambling shacks and E-Z joints. Within these places the pimps,
freeloaders, people trying to make rent money, and gamblers
congregated. They gambled away hundreds of dollars, while old-
timers kept card and domino games rolling through the night.
Soul-food restaurants established by people who used to be in the
drug business served plates of food until early morning.

Small colonies of houses shared borders with the projects.
Families from the projects who had been able to scrape up extra
money lived in these Mississippi wooden shacks with holes in the
walls and roofs.

I lived in noisy Elmer Scott, near the lake and the grade school
Jose Navarro, with babies, kids, and thousands of people. There
were two distinct groups of families. The first was those who had
minimum-wage jobs, who sacrificed and let their children eat
daily hot meals and wear decent clothing. The second was those
who had totally given up. They were thieves, hustlers, dope
dealers, and lost dreamers, like my mother. Being content with
day-to-day survival was a forced way of life.

But some people, like Ms. Ruthy Mae, didn't seem to belong
to either group. She was an older woman with two daughters in
their early twenties and Chris, her five-year-old son. She had been
in the projects a long time. She kept to herself, hardly ever going
outdoors. From her house, which had junk stacked everywhere
and an old-fashioned blow fan in the kitchen window, Ms. Ruthy

Mae gave like Jesus. She gave us butter, bread, chicken, and anything else my mother sent us to borrow. She gave us clothes, even though they had the decadent odor of a trash mine. She never turned us down unless she just didn't have it. She never spoke unkind words, never raised her voice. She wouldn't be around for long, though.

Then there were people like me, who observed every word, every facial expression, and every event. I had to know how things worked, white policemen, drug addicts, project concentration camps. I bugged everyone I thought had an answer or a clue. The torture everyone endured was as much a part of me as my own fingers, as livid as the scorch vulture.

Outdoors, the ants were still nonstop near my green pickle bucket. The ant bed, dead in the middle of the several trails that branched out from it, held the ants' harvest. No matter how far they ventured, or how difficult it was dragging a grasshopper or spider, they always faithfully returned to the nest. The ones leaving the nest seemed to be more vibrant, more energized, than the ones entering, who seemed burdened down. Antennas gesticulating, they scavenged until they found something edible to return to the queen. It was obvious that the force that drove them through death, storms, and stomps of giants was natural.

But there was a group even more loyal than the ants; and their trails to the lair were just as visible. Unlike the ants, they worked not only in the daytime, but also at night. In droves, from all directions, they would converge on the several corners where the dope dealers worked all day, pumping their product into these people. Twenty-four hours a day, seven days a week, men mostly in their early thirties accepted TVs, food stamps, clothes, and anything of value for the dope. Unlike the ants, the dope fiends were not bothered. There was no one to stomp their heads or scatter their trails, as long as they continued to come.

From my pickle bucket, while my weak body warned me that it was time to go lie down, I looked to the corner. I saw some dope dealers working. Nearby, a boy named Mooky was practicing on his tiny drum set, which his mother had saved her money to get. His mother had four children and was from the minimum-wage group. When upset, she would viciously beat poor Kevin, Mooky's older brother, even though she wasn't on drugs. Her husband had left, and she had to move to the projects. She stayed frustrated.

Mooky was about four years old. In his Salvation Army clothes, he had cocked his head to the side and was listening to the changing rhythms of the drums, as if they held the answers to every deep mystery. The steady thrums of the beats were echoing off the brick walls.

On the horizon, the sun was setting. On the ground, the ants were quitting. But the dope fiends were scampering in now from all directions, letting nothing keep them away.

"Mooky," his mom said, "it's time to stop."

On that day, I made a personal promise that if I did nothing else, I would never become like my mother or these people. I would just say no. However, I didn't realize that most of them had thought it was that simple, too. But no matter how intelligent, full of courage, motivated, and strong they had been, the ghettos, slums, and places like the projects had broken them all. Now, because my mother, my life guide, had birthed me right in the middle of the mud, the odds against my survival were stacked higher than the Empire State Building.

As a testimony to society's power, the black mothers and fathers, who could have explored space, built cities, and pioneered new medicine in America, kept coming for their dope. I wondered if just for one night the steady drum of their footsteps would end.

Black parents rose in the mornings and turned into the living dead. They traveled back and forth to the corners, where they brought the harvest and purchased heroin. They locked themselves in dank bedrooms and bathrooms. They tied straps tightly around their arms, making their veins stick out. They sucked cooked pills out of bottle tops and into needles. With the injections, release eased into their veins, their precious souls. Perhaps they glimpsed happy times, strong communities. Maybe they saw themselves holding up torches of guidance, lighting the way for their children. Maybe they felt pure courage deep within, courage they had given up. Somewhere inside were men and women of intellect and capability trying to get out. Or did they see their tasks as so overbearing until they just refused to fight? So they abandoned their pride and families, their manhood and motherhood, their responsiblity to their children. And every day they hid the shame of this refusal behind the guile of dope.

2

DEADMAN

A week or two later, still in July 1977, I stood outside, just to breathe the fresh morning air. I wanted this to be a routine early morning, one when most of the evil and the people who had not gotten enough sleep during the night, like my family, were still asleep. Leonard Brown, Ugly Biggun, stood on the porch a unit down. What had brought that rascal out this early? I hated that bully, that fourteen-year-old who beat up little kids like me. He acted like he was so bad among our ranks but would act so friendly around older, bigger guys.

Biggun was slim but strong for a fourteen-year-old. He had a wide, flat chest and ripples in his stomach. His pea-size, wrinkled head, with flaming red eyes in slit sockets, was a constant joke. Several months before, when we first moved in, Biggun had been okay. The dummy had even tried to teach me something.

"It's a simple trick," Biggun had said one day as we walked

together to the redneck store to buy a pack of Kool Lights for my mother. "All you do is take off at full speed and hold that speed until the person gets tired. Then let him get close to you. Suddenly slide into the ground, and he'll go past you."

I listened curiously as he continued. "Get up and go another direction. He'll give up; they all give up. . . . You better learn it because you'll need it around here," he had warned. If Biggun had reason to run from anything, if he couldn't scare it away with his face, I certainly had better learn the escape, I thought. I used the trick the next day, when ugly Biggun went back to being a bully and chased me down the street. But with a little improvisation of my own, I was sliding into the hard ground and kicking up a cloud of dust as he ran after me. I used his own worthless trick on him.

As I watched from my front porch, men got out of two cars and walked toward Shortleg Lee's* apartment. They were all skinny, and they all had Afros. The Afro bandits.

No matter how many times they would do it, I could never believe that men would get out of those cars and roam through here to kill somebody. Kids were around here. But here they were again. I ran into the house and peered past the shades of the living room. I was in shock, but still excited. Ugly Biggun ran into his house, too. The Afro bandits were seven strong, with pistols and pump shotguns, and one held a jar of dark liquid. It seemed they planned to catch the dope dealer Lee while he slept. His time had finally come. His workers were not in sight. But to my surprise, the Afro bandits walked past his apartment and surrounded my young friend Mark's house. They were going to kill Mark's family.

They fanned out around the front door. One of them knocked. Mark's fat, double-chinned mom answered. I ran out the door, going to get a close-up of the massacre.

"What do you want?" she asked.

"Where is Lee?" said the Afro bandit.

"Lee doesn't live here."

"Tell Lee some friends are here to see him."

"My kids are in here," she moaned in a tremulous voice. "Lee doesn't live here, I told you."

"Well, which one of these apartments does he live in?"

She lied. "I don't know."

They continued to badger Mark's mom. Meanwhile, I followed two Afros who went around to guard the back door. Soon, a third one came back there to round them up. "We've found Lee," he coldly said. I trailed them loosely.

As they were reassembling in front of Lee's apartment, two more were going around to prevent escape through the back. The head Afro knocked on Lee's door once, then twice. He waited, then knocked again. No one answered. He signaled for his men to retreat. They slowly walked backwards, maybe ten paces. Then the man holding the jar stepped forward and threw it against the upstairs window. The smell of gasoline erupted in the air as the gangly Afro men unloaded their weapons while backing slowly toward the two cars. They left in a hurry.

The minute the gunfire began, I hit the ground facedown. All children would hit the ground when they heard gunfire, as though they had been trained in the military. The gunfire sounded like a sound track from some war movie. Mark jumped from his second-story window in fear and ran for his aunt's house in Edgar Wards. Before rising up, I waited several minutes through the silence that comes after several loud explosions. The gunfire made people scramble from their apartments. Lee's splintered window frame was smoking. He emerged unharmed and walked toward the parking lot with a pistol; he knew he had to show the people he wasn't afraid, or they would lose their respect.

Shortleg Lee, a man in his early thirties, was well known, not notoriously recognized, as some dope dealers, but known, like a natural landmark, building, or park. His right leg was lame, so he dragged it when he walked. He had short napped hair and a beer belly under a flat chest. He always wore blue jeans and a T-shirt. His manner was quiet and soft-spoken, always smiling. He also was extremely secretive. Some young black woman had rented a project unit for Shortleg Lee, and that was where he spent his days.

Only his dope comrades, who worked several street corners, knew anything about him, his past, or his family. We common people were kept ignorant. But it was obvious Lee had money, a lot of money. He bought his twenty-one-year-old girlfriend a new Mercedes-Benz. But he didn't openly flaunt his money or carry it in big wads like the few younger dealers. He captured the people's yearning for money in another, insidious way.

For example, if you told Lee your age on your birthday, he would give you a crisp new dollar bill for each year you had lived. If you were fifteen, you would receive fifteen dollars. We kids wouldn't utter one word when police tried to pick us for information about him. We were loyal to Shortleg Lee's money.

One Christmas morning, Shortleg had his workers deliver fat hams to all the parents and expensive toys to all the children near his unit—about three hundred people. Our block lit up like a street festival that day, for Lee also had his workers and their women prepare a tasty feast, with music, dancing, and drinks, on his decorated front yard. Everyone treated Lee like some sort of Godfather.

After the attempt on his life, Lee kept a squadron of men near and around him. He became more secretive than before, only staying in his project unit a few days concurrently. But he never stopped selling dope while living in the projects, and he was never caught there.

After the shoot-out, I went back home and explained what had happened to my family. My mother told me never to run toward danger again. She was high. Sherrie and Junior sensed the inevitable and darted from the room like roaches when you flip on a kitchen light. But I remained, pondering the shoot-out; I just couldn't believe people could do that in this neighborhood. Then, my mother screamed in her early morning, rough voice: "I need someone to go to the store for me." My sister and brother had sensed this, but I had been distracted. It tickled me to see how alert they had become about getting out of trips to the store. But there was no way I could get out of this one, which I knew would be for cigarettes.

"Can I eat first?" I asked.

"No! Now hurry up, boy, before I beat your ass."

Unafraid, I walked to her and got the money. I went out the back door.

Another whooping probably would not have bothered me. My hide was getting used to them. Sometimes I would turn to look at her, dry-eyed, as she hammered her blows across my back, legs, and buttocks, just to let her see the anger in my face.

During times like this day, when my mother was in a bad mood, I didn't mind going to the store. It was a way to avoid her. If avoiding her meant just hanging around all day without eating, we would do it. Beatings, accompanied by loud shouting and cursing, were a way to release frustration. Every kid I knew received these whoopings. Sometimes, up and down the noisy streets, the kids yelled and screamed, "Okay, Momma, I won't do it no moa."

And we children didn't just receive our whoopings at home. Some of us were beat in our front yards or in the middle of a street. I hated the beatings that woke me from my sleep. It was difficult enough going to sleep. As I had, some children had been made to take their whoopings standing wet and naked after leaving the shower. It borderlined on torture.

A redneck white family owned a store where sons of the owner wore guns like wild cowboys and charged ludicrous prices for everything. So everyone shopped at the nearby shopping center, which had two grocery stores, a Laundromat, and several department stores. Cigarettes were too expensive at the redneck store. They cost a mere dollar and five cents at the Tom Thumb. So I took the hidden trail along the lake to get there.

Along the trail, a route I would walk a thousand times, I tossed pebbles into the calm lake, which was maybe a half mile long and wide, with cattails and shrubbery growing along its edge. The trail veered down near the water, where snakes lounged in the cotton trees and bushes. After getting back on the concrete of the street, I entered the shopping center, which had a parking lot the size of a football field. Walking around the crowds on the sidewalk near department store facades, I mentally prepared to see Syrup Head at the Tom Thumb. She was there every day.

She eased toward me like a shy little girl. "Do you have a cigarette?" she would say, nothing more, nothing less. Her hair looked like a swarm of termites with creepy, ugly kinks in it, and she never wore shoes on her crusty feet. People in Elmer Scott who knew Syrup Head said heroin had driven her crazy when she was young.

She used to live in the George Loving section, which was so foreign to me that it could have been another country. She had been a fierce fiend: first cigarettes, then weed, then heroin. On Rupert Street, in Edgar Wards, she had openly sold her body simply to share someone's dope, even as a teenager, and desperate men who wanted cheap sex had abused her that way. But one day she had threatened to call the police on a dealer after he refused to give her credit. Wanting to get rid of her, he had laced her heroin capsule. Now, in her thirties, she remembered only her very first chemical habit, cigarettes.

Three Finger Willie was also at the Tom Thumb that morning. He had been given this nickname because his left hand had three fingers missing. He looked like a pencil with a black wig where the eraser should have been. People rumored that he was an ax murderer. He would stand in front of the store, swinging at invisible objects. I dreaded going to the store when he was there; the thought of dismembered and mutilated bodies, especially mine, horrified me more than any shoot-out. I avoided him and bought the cigarettes.

While my mother lay on the living room couch, smoking her

cigarettes, I fixed a bowl of rice, being careful to rinse all the roach eggs from the bowl, and a glass of water. There was nothing else to eat. When she was done with her cigarette, my mother came into the kitchen.

"I'll be back in a while. Wash those dishes up. Tell Sherrie I said to cut up and fry that chicken."

"But, Momma, it's not my time to wash dishes," I argued, as I always did, even when it was my time.

"I said wash those dishes. Now shut up talking back."

After she left, I heard the usual rumble that signaled my brother's approach. I looked out the back door. He was making his daily rounds in his shopping basket. Several kids had squeezed under the blanket.

"Junior, go tell Sherrie Momma said to come cut this chicken up."

"You go tell her," he screamed back. He hurried around the corner and was gone. I began to wash the dishes.

Another sink full of pots and pans, roach eggs and roach wings. I dreaded this. Every day that's all my brother, sister, and I did was wash, scrub, and slave for Momma. These were not ordinary chores a woman would give her child. One thing about my mother, heroin made her want the entire house cleaned, meticulously, from top to bottom. Whenever she was high, the cleaning came before everything, eating, doing homework, even sleeping. If one of us went to bed without washing dishes, he or she could expect to be awakened: with a belt, shoe, extension cord, stick, broom, lamp, or fist. "Wash out Momma's panties, massage Momma's neck." And if I said no, the cool words "Do it for Momma" and "That's Momma's baby boy" did me in every time. Kindness was so rare.

When she wasn't high, the dishes usually would sit in the sink for weeks. The kitchen was creepy. The rusty shelves, where sewage plumbing stuck out, were filthy. Our pots went there. Too many roaches and rats, alive and dead, were under there, too. No matter how hard I tried, I just never could get all the grime, chicken skin, and food from the pots. So I let them sit filled with water on the cabinet. I was taking a chance because if she came back disappointed, I would get a whooping.

To find Sherrie, I walked over to the next unit, where her friend Teresa* lived. Her family was a replica of my own, with a brother, a sister, and a heroin momma who slaved her like my mother did my sister. Knocking on the back door, I called to Sherrie, "Momma said come and cut the chicken up."

"Dog, she make me sick, always running off and expect me to cook. They ain't my kids," she said when she came out, referring to my brother and me.

She always acted rebellious around Teresa; but I knew she didn't mean any harm toward us. She came anyway.

"Teresa, I'll be back later," she said. I walked ahead of her, giving her privacy if she wanted to whisper some stuff.

Onward our lives went during 1977 and 1978, still our first or second year in the projects, washing roach dishes, running from bullies, cutting up chickens. Around then, my mother started having men come over and stay in her room. She usually came from in there high, and after several months of her lying, claiming they were only friends, I put things together. I really knew the truth when I heard women say my mother shouldn't do that in front of her kids and heard kids call my mother a bitch to my face. I let her think I was ignorant, though, so that she could preserve her dignity. But I despised every man that came over to take advantage of my poor mother. I let them know it, too, through looks, snarls, frowns, and much later with fists and knives. The ones who stayed awhile, some weeks, some months, earned my respect.

Most of the time, though, the men would not stay. This meant that there constantly was a different man as a father in our lives. You can imagine how confused we became as children. The minute we adapted to the new one, he was replaced by another one. For women like my mother, there was an unspoken rule that said you had to take the kids along with the woman. Some of the men would feign interest in us to adhere to this. Others she saw were really sincere, I think.

Of all the men she would meet, I was most impressed with Pie. He was short, thick, and wore a beard. Since he was from Oak Cliff, a black neighborhood south of the projects, he knew little about project life. Even though he was in his late twenties, he still lived at home, where we visited only once. His mother hated the idea of him being with a woman who had three kids.

But my mother, regardless, still could attract a good man. So, eventually, he moved in and became our father. Pie quickly took responsibility for teaching Junior and me during the few months he lived with us. He taught us how to make up our beds, fold sheets, and sort laundry. He made sure we got up on time to go to school. He would sit me under his arm, where I could watch my heroes, the Dallas Cowboys, play football—every TV in the projects would be tuned to the Cowboys' games. At the first meeting of father and sons, he introduced us to personal hygiene. Afterward I was so excited I took a bath with Comet and washed the tub out with soap. He had meant vice versa.

The one and only Christmas that Pie spent with us, he woke Junior and me up early Christmas morning. "Get up, boys," he said in his plain, reserved way. "I have something to show you." I figured he had gotten us some of those Salvation Army green, wooden toys, the kind every child knew and hated, so I wasn't all that excited. But Pie had done more, had gone to the limits to make us happy. He held his hands over my eyes, while burying Junior's face in his hip, and guided us down the stairs. Once we made it into the living room, he uncovered our eyes and let us take a look. When my vision adjusted, I saw the hottest toy that year, a cops-and-robbers racetrack, which Pie had already assembled on the hard tile.

"So you think y'all a be happy with that?" Pie asked, smiling. Then, as Junior and I dove for the track, he let out a hearty laugh, the first and last one I ever heard from him. Since it was still six in the morning, we played until we fell asleep, sometimes Pie joining in, right there on the floor. He would leave us at times to help my mother put the finishing touches on the big Christmas meal we would gorge on later. In time our sister woke and began feverishly to unwrap her new clothes and games. Later that evening, my brother and I walked around the house looking like we had swallowed bowling balls, from the three or four plates we'd eaten.

But there was only so much Pie could do for us in a couple of months before things turned bad. Money eventually came up missing, valuables misplaced. Pie and my mother often got into shouting matches. One day she threw a glass at him as he stood at the bottom of the stairs; that event marked the end of their relationship. He moved out a week later. If Pie had stayed, he could have helped us become one of the minimum-wage families.

But other men, I learned in 1978, were out just to take advantage of a weak, unschooled woman. It didn't matter, though; every new man she had we called Daddy. That's how bad we longed for a father figure, then, at our young ages. None of them was worth a damn. Some of them I despised. One of them, Charles*, hit her, a woman, in the face.

It happened after the project authorities transferred us to another unit, so that they could remodel the former one. By then her temper had become so bad that she would scratch and claw the men when she became upset. Charles, who lived with his mother several blocks away, was in his early twenties. He had been visiting our bare apartment often and locking himself away with my mother. One day, while I stood in the door and watched, she and Charles wrestled in her bedroom. She tried to pick his eyes out. He angrily pinned her to the bed and tightly gripped her neck. Suddenly he reached back with his right fist and slammed it into her face, twice. She let out a high-pitched wail. Before I could react, he darted past me down the stairs and fled through some empty apartments.

She lay there holding her eye and moaning. Then she turned toward me and pointed. "What kind of a son are you, stand there and let your momma get beat up? Get out! Get out!" she screamed.

I ran to the kitchen, got the biggest butcher knife I could find, and ran after Charles. But he had disappeared.

I wouldn't see him until years later, when I was a young teenager carrying guns. I saw him walking, though he didn't recognize me. I was finally gonna give him what he deserved, a bullet in the head for busting up my mother. He wouldn't know where it came from. My anger was building as I followed him for two or three blocks. I was about to shoot him, in broad daylight. But grace was with him that day, because I simply changed my mind and went the other way.

In only those two years, my mother had become completely fettered by the projects. She had turned into a complete drug addict and whore, and her addiction had reached a higher level. Her arm was swallowing up pills like quicksand. Odds were if we stayed around the house, we would get a whooping. My brother never cared about these odds, since he was always the first one up and out. Until school started, he would just push his buggy all day and not come home until nightfall. His plan had worked fairly well; only once or twice did grotesque Biggun chase him home. Nothing was at home anyway. We had gotten down to having jelly-and-syrup sandwiches for dinner.

At home, I wasn't too concerned with my mother, either. She couldn't fuss at who she couldn't find. Since she hardly came in my room, since she never came among that filth—it probably would have killed her—I just stayed in the closet. When she called my name, I would ignore her. I would sit in there all day, fighting off the insects and remaining motionless if she stuck her head in the bedroom door. I enjoyed the total darkness in the closet, away from most of the noise, the dope, and the fussing.

That closet, my sanctuary, my friend. I would just daydream in there, sometimes thinking about my dad, hoping he would come and visit us. But he didn't, not once.

From the closet, I would also keep the window open, in case I heard the other kids rounding up everyone for a game of Deadman. I would wait until my mother went inside her room, then dart out the door. One evening, only weeks after we had started starving in that Hitler camp, only months after men had started seeing my mother, a special game of Deadman got under way.

"Who-all wanna play Deadman?" one kid asked.

"Ooh, I do."

"I do, too."

"Go and get Chris, Mark, Ke-Ke, Donkey, Ping Head, Big-gun, and his sister Scootie," and another dozen children, which was easy because we were so many and because everyone loved Deadman. All frictions, all jealousies, left when we played Deadman. It seemed sacred. Moreover, we children were too anxious because of the excitement about to happen. For Deadman was a complex game, full of ways in which the players could be entrapped, ensnared, eliminated, or become a Deadman. It was just like living in the projects.

Huddled close together in a circle, like a crowd trying to stay warm in a winter storm, everyone held his fist at chest level. Ping Head, Biggun's brother, used the counting technique to determine who would be the first Deadman. "I struck a match and the match went out." (Whoever's fist he stopped on would lower that hand.) One person dropped a fist. "I struck a match and the match went out." Another person dropped a fist. This continued until one of Biggun's fists remained. Since he was the only person with a fist still held up, he was the Deadman.

He had to catch and touch the other children, who, in turn, would help him catch the others, until the last person was captured. This person, whose fists never remained after he had finished counting because of the counting formula, would huddle everyone up and count again.

An entire project block of twenty-four buildings was the area where the manhunt took place. It was getting dark, the best time for playing because it wasn't so hot. Across from my unit stood two vacant, vandalized buildings—in a few spots throughout a project block would always be several vacant units. All the windows had been broken out of these. Glass, nails, and pieces of Sheetrock were everywhere. Holes had been kicked through the walls so that a man could walk through each apartment or could crawl or hide in the ceiling. It looked like a construction site.

Biggun stood outside the circle of people, waiting to touch anyone who tried to run. In time, one person dashed away. When Biggun took off after her, the whole circle scattered in all directions. The acrobatic youngsters headed toward the ghostly project buildings, while the sprinters stayed in the open space. The others went to find hiding places somewhere on the vast project block.

I climbed the tree that grew in front of a vacant project unit, our Deadman play area. Eric, a kid who loved this game, dove through a window. His mom and dad worked for dope dealers, and he was terrified of staying in his house, since many parents who worked for dope dealers were being found shot to death inside their apartments.

Biggun dove out the window behind Eric; but Eric was too quick for him. Several others whom Biggun already had touched ran after Eric as he ran back inside the building. The whole spectacle was open to me from the tall tree I was sitting in, which was in jumping distance of the two-story roof. Playing Deadman, I would jump onto the roof if someone climbed up the tree behind me. If they had the courage to follow me, I would hang from the roof and drop to one of the ledges, then jump from it and escape through the building. When Biggun climbed the tree, I jumped.

After running through the project, I blasted down to the other end of the block to get far away from Biggun.

Deadman, all the kids loved to play it, all the adults loved to watch it. They would set chairs outdoors to watch the game for hours. Ms. Betty, Mrs. Burnese, Ms. Brown, loved to see the kids scare the hell out of them by jumping from two-story buildings or doing flips through windows. Sometimes even the dope dealers would watch. One-arm Nathan*, whose arm had been amputated, a man who kept his dope in a medicine bottle hidden in nearby bushes, in a crack between the sidewalk, or in his empty sleeve. Or Messy Marvin (before he was murdered in a hotel room), who had a big house in the suburbs with a gun collection in his living room.

I thought I had outsmarted Biggun by running to the other end of the block. It was getting dark, so everybody else was staying near the vacant units, near people and the older boys. I ran between the two units where we had lived, now vacant on the other end of the block. Biggun's figure was gaining on me. Evidently I hadn't gotten around the building fast enough. I increased my speed, preparing for the slide move. Just as Biggun was upon me, I faked the slide; but he didn't go for the bait. He grabbed and threw me to the ground. He was going to get his revenge for my outsmarting him with his own trick earlier, despite the sacredness of the Deadman game. With his knee in my back, he grabbed for my pants, and tried to pull them down. What the hell was Biggun doing? I wrestled onto my back and looked into his face. He wasn't Biggun. He wasn't one of the Deadman children. He was a rapist.

I screamed for help from that little dark spot between two tall project buildings, screamed until the rapist got scared and ran off. He probably knew the projects were too crowded, knew the dope fiends stayed too busy. He knew if the dope dealers heard my screams, they would have stomped him until every drop of life drained from his body.

I breathed a sigh of relief as I stood and dusted the dirt from my pants. I was so glad that this rapist hadn't succeeded, because I already had been through the experience. Before we moved into the projects, when my mother and father were still together, a young man had shown a strange interest in me. I must have been under five because I was not yet in any school.

With the promise of some candy, he took me into a shed and made me pull my pants down. I don't recall any pain, so I don't think he entered me physically but had his privacy between my legs. Afterward the boy said he wanted me to come back. And though I really didn't understand, I felt something was very wrong. So I told my dad, without telling him what had happened. I didn't want to go back. The next time my dad saw the boy, he shouted to him to leave me alone. Later we moved away.

That spring of 1978, I walked home and didn't tell anyone what had happened between those two dark buildings. It wasn't the first time some rapists had tried that, and it wouldn't be the last. I went back to the safety of my closet, among the lifeless clothes. I hated living here, among all the bullies, noise, and murder. I hated starving, hated cleaning up like a maid and washing out panties in the bathroom face bowl. I hated my father for abandoning me, with an eight-year-old's hate, which, of course, never lasted long. Just because he left my mother didn't mean he had to leave his children, too.

3

COOL BROTHER

By the summer of 1978, I had already begun to develop strong self-reliance traits. I was coming to grips with my reality. We were children in abject poverty, separated from real America. We had parents who were trying every morning to deal with the man or woman in the mirror. The first law of nature, self-preservation, prevailed for them. They became wrapped up in big balls of grief and left us to fend for ourselves. But my mother, even in her zombielike condition, was there when I needed her the most.

She would come out of her dope trance, utter her powerful wisdom, then disappear without a trace: "Don't hang around the wrong crowd. Don't stay out too late." Times like that made me wonder how my mother would have been if she had not been put through so much, if her mother had let her go to school, and if the father of her children had not abandoned her.

When she confronted me about stealing food from the shopping center, mother's intuition, she explained in two quick sentences, nothing more, nothing less, how it could devastate my life:

"Jerrold, whatever I do, I'm not gonna raise you to be no thief. When people find out you're a thief, they'll never trust you again."

But I was driven by hunger and had no concern for what others thought. I had experienced enough hunger headaches to know that you can't do anything when you're cramping and swelling and every cell in your body is screaming for a bread crumb or something. It almost paralyzes you.

The boy who introduced me to stealing, Bad Baby, was sixteen, short, and lean. He was aggressive, and would act quickly on his beliefs, which were good ones. The young girls loved his long Afro and the sharp clothes his mother, who had a speech defect, piled up for him. Of course they were a minimum-wage family, and they lived next door. Their apartment had nice cheap furniture, pictures, pots, plants, and wall-to-wall carpeting on the floor. The apartment also stayed cool and pleasant from the air conditioner in the window.

"Jerrold, are you coming over for dinner?" Bad Baby often asked.

"Naw, man, I'm not hungry," my shame would say.

"Come on over and eat, Jerrold. There's no reason to be ashamed, little brother. Ain't nothing wrong with eating at a friend's house."

Bad Baby had this kind of sympathy for my brother and me because even the poorest kids now talked about how dirty and ragged we were. They had given us nicknames. They called me Dirt Dobbler and Junior Dirt Mieser. But Bad Baby wasn't like them. Instead, he did nice things and never talked bad about me.

Bad Baby was also good at building bicycles from used parts. He also stole them. At times, when his mother let him, he would ride his bike out of the neighborhood. I didn't have a bike of my own, like kids from the minimum-wage group, so he would carry me along on the back of his bike. We went to visit his aunt across Hampton. We ran errands to the store. But on one trip, Bad Baby took me across the Hampton bridge. It was the first time.

With Prescott, Bad Baby's older brother, we rode alongside the traffic on busy Hampton Road until we came upon a residential area. As we turned down several different streets, Bad Baby and Prescott checking in all directions, I noticed small bikes, toys, and chairs unattended on their front lawns. They stopped at one corner, where Bad Baby ushered me off and pointed to a bike lying in someone's front yard.

He said, "Jerrold, this is the only way you'll ever have a bike. Go get it, man."

"I don't want to," I told him.

He and Prescott stepped away for a second, talked, and returned.

"Jerrold, you'll never have a bike unless you do it this way," he lectured.

"Bad Baby, take me home."

"If you don't get the bike, we're gonna leave you here."

Seeing that I wasn't budging, they sped off. I ran after them, but they were too fast. Scared, I turned back around, hopped on the bike, and pedaled in the direction they had ridden. They stood around the corner, waiting for me. We hurried back past the traffic and back across the bridge. Along the way, Bad Baby told me that the people had plenty of money and would never miss the bike. To keep me from being whooped, he told my mom he'd built it for me. And I kept it.

Bad Baby had always observed what went on at our house and had always been concerned. So it was no surprise when he found out my mother was on drugs. After he gradually became closer to my brother and me, he convinced us to run away and sneak into his house late one night, even though it was only next door. He thought things would be better if my mom was reported.

Since our mother had traded the upstairs room with Junior and me, Bad Baby had to creep onto the ledge under our window and above the back door. After he was inside, he tucked clothes under our blankets to look like sleeping people, and helped us out the window. The next day, authorities from Human Resources came. This funny-looking white man, dressed in a suit, took us to our apartment. He identified himself to our mother and told her he alone would question my brother and me. She gave him a nervous "okay" and looked at us sadly, as if she knew her wrongdoing had finally caught up with her. Before the white man started, I whispered to my brother to tell the man we were okay. My brother looked disappointed, as though I were messing up his chance to get away from the Hitler camp.

As for me, I had gone along reluctantly with Bad Baby's plan, but this was too much. From snatches of conversations at the corners with the dope dealers I had heard about these strange white people from the state who destroy black families. I had been warned to avoid them at all costs. But more than any verbal admonishment, my instincts compelled me not to trust them, especially after the policemen. She was my mother. This was our home.

In our room with the door shut, the man began, talking with that soft, soothing voice, the kind psychiatrists use to relax people. "Now, I don't want you to be afraid of what will happen to you boys, because no one's gonna hurt you. I just want you to tell me the truth, and I'll see if I can make things better for you, okay?"

"Okay," my brother said, already falling under the spell. But I was not to be taken. The white man began his questions.

"Now, does your mother feed you?"

"Yes, sir," I said quickly. "We eat very well."

"How often do you attend school?"

"Ooh, we rarely miss days. I love school, my momma always helps me."

"Does she take care of your sister?"

"Yes, sir."

"Does she do drugs?"

"Ooh, no, sir," I told him.

The white man started looking confused, as if he couldn't understand why neighbors would report something wrong with such happy kids and such a good mother. Before leaving, he apologized to my mother. And we never heard from the state people again.

Thereafter, I was forbidden from talking with Bad Baby. Before the summer ended, he and his family moved across Hampton to the shack houses. I later learned that Prescott, Bad Baby's brother, was murdered there. His throat was cut.

My quiet brother, who also was experimenting with self-reliance, had learned to steal during his own adventures in the Hitler camp. And together, on days when our humger would not let us rest, we stole food from the shopping center. We stole things that were easy to conceal, like cans of sardines and small packages of rice. A bowl of rice and a tall glass of water was enough for our indiscriminate stomachs.

Another hustle we used to get food was going into the shopping center late at night to steal TV guides. The newspaper companies dumped hundreds of papers on the sidewalk. So Mark (the one who had jumped from his window to avoid the Afro hitmen), another kid named Big Mark, my brother, and I would get there about one in the morning. We would quickly sift through the piles and pick out all the TV guides. Then, when we had gathered all we could carry, we would scurry back to the lake to take the hidden trail. Back in the projects, we would go from door to door, selling our magazines for a quarter apiece.

We weren't thieves, just hungry children. Work, when we

could find it, took the place of stealing. Each morning Junior and I would rise early and go looking for jobs, walking up Industrial, up Singleton, up Hampton Road. Consumed with our attempts to find work, we would stay gone all day without eating. Most places would not hire us because we were too young, just eight and ten-year-olds. Occasionally we did stumble upon a place that needed temporary help. And my brother once landed a job for a service station that paid him about thirty dollars for a full week of work.

We worked at the shopping center, too. All day my brother and I would stand at the Tom Thumb with Syrup Head and Three Finger Willie, roaming around. We would ask customers if we could carry their groceries but would not ask for a fee. Instead we would just stand there, looking dirty and hungry. When we were done, some would tip us, others wouldn't. We could make a good seven bucks after a long ten-hour day. We gave our mother sometimes all, sometimes half the money; the rest we spent on food or candy. We also dug through the trash cans behind the DAV store in the shopping center, looking for clothes, toys, change, and good pairs of shoes.

I still played Deadman, but not as often because a body had been found in the Deadman vacant units. Between the stealing and scavenging, though, I was managing to stay away from the house, where things weren't getting any better. A bootleg family had moved in next door to us. They bought cases of beer from south Dallas, a wet part of the city, and stored it in their house. From their back door they sold each can for a dollar. Nighttime traffic was steady in and out of their house. On the corners, the heroin dealers were in full force.

I was on my Huffy bike all the time now. I often rode it down Fishtrap and Shaw streets, near the two candy trucks, and on Apple Grove and Morris, up and down the sidewalks and trails on the block, not stopping for the common fistfights that crowds gathered to watch or the young boys burning mattress cotton at nightfall to keep the mosquitoes away.

I would even ride my bike where the rapists had attacked me. Each time I did, a black man sitting on a porch watched me curiously. Sometimes a woman was with him. I made a mental note to keep an eye on him. If he were another rapist, I would not be his next victim.

Riding my bike on the other end of the block, I grew closer to Eric, a boy I played Deadman with. He and I were the same age and both had heroin mothers so we had a lot in common. Eric was afraid to live in his house, a problem he discussed with me. He knew something bad was going to happen there. So, he told me, he kept his bedroom window open, in case he needed to make the two-story jump to safety. He dreamed, he often said, of the day when his parents would stop selling dope and they all could leave the projects forever. To pass the time, we would sit out at night on the swings the authorities had built. We would swing our souls away late into the dark, starry nights. Both our young mothers had stopped coming home.

Eric also knew of the muscular, dark man who had been watching me. I pointed him out one day while he sat on Eric's porch. Eric was surprised. He said that the man had been with some of the prettiest women in the projects. He was no rapist. He was one of those settled cool brothers, the smooth ones who know a lot about women.

One evening, instead of going up Morris, I rode past the man's house, where he was sitting on the porch with his girlfriend. He stopped me and asked what my name was, said he knew about my mother and my home situation. He said he used to be just like me when he was a boy. Looking into my eyes with his own black rubies, he told me I was good-looking.

"Women will take care of you when you're older, if you know how to move a woman's heart," he said. His girlfriend just sat there and smiled. The man wasn't threatening, and he aroused my curiosity, too much for me not to go back. So I did go, all summer long.

I don't think he had children because I never saw any. I know he didn't work. The apartment, which belonged to his woman, was sparsely furnished and had only two dining chairs and a couch. It was still a project unit, so it had the small rooms, which stayed hot. Everything was kept tidy and clean, even the tile floors, which required a lot of mopping. His backyard had the same wire clotheslines and red ants.

He kept food, a lot of vegetables, greens, and fish, but none of the disgusting pig feet, pig ears, and things my mother cooked from time to time. He never fried his food and said he didn't eat pork because it was worse than putting heroin in your blood. He, not his girlfriend, cooked their meals; I found that odd. Until he moved away, he gave me food, which I ate like a starved animal.

But what I recall most is his bedroom. The windows were covered by heavy blankets, forever blackening the sun. It stayed totally dark in there. A dull, red light, like one blinking on a dark stormy night atop a tall tower, revealed the shadow of a small table next to his bed. That light and the reefer smoke gave the room an enchanted setting.

While the deep rhythms of the band Parliament and Bootsy's Rubber Band softly played out of four speakers in each corner of the room, I would sit, light-headed from his reefer smoke, absorbing the almost spiritual music, and listen to this black man, who wore a net cap over his small Afro. I clearly remember two of his imperatives: "Always love your woman's mind," and, "You have to take care of her, so she'll hold you up when the white man wants to crush you." Not until years later would I come to understand his advice or the rare kind of black man he was. Over time I grew to respect him, because unlike many of us, he seemed content and at peace, seemed to know some secrets about the projects, perhaps their purpose, perhaps why we were in them, that made him seem not subdued, at least in many ways.

After the sweet brother piqued my interest in women, it wasn't long before I met my first female friend, Gloria*, on the day she and her family moved to west Dallas, near my unit, on the row behind Biggun's. My friendship with Eric had been dwindling away naturally, like friendships between little kids do, so Gloria came along on time.

From the first day I saw her at the candy truck on Fishtrap, Gloria was beautiful to me. Too beautiful. She was thin, her skin gleamed with natural health, and her eyes were pearls, shadowed by shoulder-length hair. Not even her old clothes and weathered shoes could overshadow her beauty. After I gathered enough courage I introduced myself.

"My name is Jerrold, you must don't live around here."

"How'd you know?" she asked.

"Because you're shopping at the high candy truck. If you want to, I'll show you where the cheap one is."

"That'll be nice," she said, looking as if she knew she had met her first friend. And from that day forward, that's the way Gloria and I would get along, simply, openly, and cheerfully.

I walked her back home from the candy truck and offered to help her and her family move in.

With the work of moving, Gloria was helping as much as her girlish strength would allow, carrying bags of clothes and boxes of pots over the barren ground between much needed rest periods. Her sisters, on the other hand, were bulky, strong women who could help the men carry the heavy pieces. They all worked under the admiration of the older boys, who stood around watching. Enough of them already had volunteered. And her mom, who was thin like Gloria, helped also.

Over time I learned that Gloria's two sisters had babies and her mother was on heroin. I didn't know much about her father—who mostly stayed to himself—except that he had a job somewhere and was the only support the family had. Gloria's mother shouted at him all the time. He seemed to be on heroin, too.

I admired the young girls as much as I could at that age, but Gloria was beyond them all because she was kind, gentle, and sweet, all at the same time. I can't recall ever hearing one bitter word come from her mouth or one angry expression on her face. The older boys longed for her ripeness through lusty stares. But of all, she liked scrawny me.

She was my first intimate contact with a woman. To share feelings and play games became the order of the day. And though we would not see each other for weeks or months, we would still say that we were going together. We would sit around together and talk on her back porch, of course after I climbed the tall tree back there, which was equally as important. Sometimes we held hands, being sure to stay away from the minimum-wage group, who would have teased us. We occasionally sat alone under the dark nights. We kissed only once, and I thought I experienced a little bit of that healing my cool friend had talked about, for even at that age blacks were real mature about relationships between men and women.

Sometimes Gloria would express her disappointment at her mother, who she thought could do a lot better. I would overhear Gloria questioning her mother about women things. But her mother, who didn't want to be bothered, always responded un- kindly, angrily, sometimes frantically. Something else I picked up on was Gloria's serious weakness. She lacked self-reliance, something all the kids had learned was vitally necessary. I hoped Gloria also would gain the skill, in time.

But for now she looked to her mother for guidance, to shape her into the fine woman she was destined to be. Gloria was enduring the projects the way my brother had when he first arrived: remaining quiet, sweet, and sensitive, even to her mother. No need to worry about Gloria, her loveliness would see her through.

Toward the end of the year 1978, however, I let Biggun and his sister Scootie peer-pressure me into picking a fight with Gloria. I wanted to be accepted by the bully, even at the cost of my love. I figured this was the better long-term investment, an example of those self-reliance skills. After he dared me, I walked up to Gloria, her knowing all along what was going on, and blackened her eye.

Biggun and Scootie oohed and aawed and giggled. But Gloria, devastated, was crying softly. When she walked away from me that day, I saw the pain and hurt in her eyes. She wouldn't speak to me for weeks; and Biggun still chased me home. I felt terrible for months afterward. But Gloria eventually forgave me. She stopped me one day as I walked in front of her house and told me I was wrong for doing that. But when I apologized, she smiled. Regardless, we would never become close friends again. Gloria and her family would soon leave the projects. Her mother was about to have a nervous breakdown.

After apologizing to Gloria that day, I went home and found a small crowd gathered across from my window. They were watching as a black man was being wheeled from the Deadman units by paramedics. A sheet hid his face. He was Gloria's father.

4

SCHOOL TORTURE

W ake up, Jerrold and Junior," Sherrie screamed early one Monday morning. There was no need to wake up. Too nervous to get some sleep, I had lain awake half the night. I forced myself out of bed and moved the broken closet door aside. A pile of dirty clothes lay just inside the closet. Sifting through the pile, I managed to find an outfit that wasn't so abhorrent. The shirt was from the early sixties, the pants dirt-packed. And my mother, she didn't even get out of bed to bid us a horrible good-bye.

That morning, Junior and Sherrie were being bussed to middle school in a white neighborhood. I had attended George Washington Carver but was being transferred to John J. Pershing. At Carver, the teachers would come and get me out of class to give me reading and spelling tests, though it didn't dawn on me until years later why they never made the other kids take so many tests. They were detecting things.

I walked reluctantly to the corner of Fishtrap and Morris, across from the graveyard. Eric wasn't out here, as I expected. He probably didn't have the nerve to put up with this mess on the first day, the hardest day. I understood him all too well. I made a mental note to tell him how things went.

On the corner, a few young kids were decent, well dressed, and from the minimum-wage group, just slightly more fortunate than I was. But all of us looked as if we had spent the night battling: drained and lifeless. Maybe the bus would have a wreck, I hoped. Maybe it would forget our street. The big yellow machine rounding the corner spoiled that idea. We children formed a single line as the bus lurched to a stop in front of us. I was nervous and embarrassed as I boarded. I was on my own.

The bus turned right on Goldman and left on Bickers, then left from Bickers onto Hampton Road. Hampton led to the long bridge. Some of the children marveled at the deep valley of grass, shrubbery, and trees alongside the Trinity River, which flowed out of sight on both sides. Others kids remained deathly quiet as they rode across the bridge. Hampton turned into Inwood Road. As we descended on this end of the bridge, a remarkable change took place.

I had heard rumors of the place we now headed toward, about all the luxury. Yet no foreknowledge could have prepared me, or any of the children, for what lay ahead. We were being bussed to the heart of the white neighborhoods, the heart of white America. They were making us go to school there.

Farther down Inwood, I noticed that the buildings were all pleasant and new. There were a lot of pretty cars. We drove farther. Nice, new, and clean houses, though not very large, started appearing along clean streets and parks, parks lush with green and healthy trees. And to my amazement, I saw tennis courts in a public park.

We came around a curve. I saw the biggest house. You could have placed half a project block on its front yard alone. It resembled a castle. There was a long, curved road leading up to its

front door and circling back out the other side. Who could have
lived in that place? It was unlike anything I had ever seen.

Some of the houses were monumental, spacious, and sculp-
tured, unlike the shack units back home in the Hitler camp. For
three project units, which could hold twenty-four families, north
Dallas had one house.

The kids lit up like Christmas trees when they saw the homes.
They exchanged awed expressions and pointed at the castles. I
was overcome, too, because I could not believe that only one
family would occupy one of these large houses. For as long as I
was bussed across the bridge, through white luxury, I would
never fail to be amazed by the homes.

John J. Pershing was a small public school. It was surrounded
by forested lots and more castle homes. In the back was a large
playground area. After the school buses parked along the curb at
the front, I went inside to enroll in the fourth grade.

As everyone was ushered into the school auditorium to be
sorted out, the blacks and whites avoided one another as if the
opposite had smallpox. During the day, everyone filled out forms
and free lunch papers and learned his classes. I tried to stay alone
in a corner. And for the first time, over the busy, yapping
schoolchildren, I missed being back home in the projects. I didn't
want to be here, among all these strange people and humiliation.
I thanked God when, after doing the paperwork, they let us go
home early.

The first day after school, walking around the corner of my
brick project unit felt like wandering on the plains of heaven. I
would continue to feel this solace after leaving the white schools
each day, all year long. The same pattern every year, pressure in
the morning, relief in the evening. I seriously was smiling that
day, happy to be back among the madness, until I saw a red-eyed
dope fiend come running around the corner with an armful of
clothes. Another one soon followed him, carrying a lamp. I knew
this meant that only one thing was in progress, and according to

the direction from which the fiends had come, it was happening to somebody I knew. Only one thing left to do: go see which poor family the project authorities were evicting this time.

Leading there, clothes and cheap furnishings littered the path. There was something peculiar about these articles of clothing. But I couldn't quite put things together, not until I arrived in back of the unit where the tree grew to the rooftop, where I had sat on the concrete porch and talked with the first girl who kissed me, who touched me, even though it was only a small, undetectable fire. What had they done to Gloria?

They had sent ten big authority workers inside Gloria's house to get her family's possessions and set them on the street curb. That was how the operation went: If a family, for whatever reason, was required to move, and if they hadn't met the deadline, big black gorilla men, authority workers, would put them out. This was all too customary in the projects.

Gloria had already left, sent to live with a relative. Small Mark was standing nearby, smirking. Gloria's family dilemma was funny to him. Mark should have known better, having had gunmen surround his house before, forcing him to jump from his window. But this was sad to me and other project people, who were trying to help load Gloria's and her family's stuff onto a truck. Yeah, Mark thought this disaster was really a laugh, a major joke. But the other news he later shared with me—about which he didn't feel so humorous—wiped that dumb smile from his face. Probably hit too close to home. Eric's parents had been murdered.

The dope dealing had caught up with them. They had turned in only half the money and couldn't come up with the rest. And that very morning, two men had kicked down their project door and killed. They had shot at little Eric, too, as he ran out the back door. Later, one of Eric's relatives had come and taken him away, which explained why he didn't show for school. I felt sorry for Eric. Though it was a terrible price to pay, he had finally gotten out.

44

A week later, I had settled in at John J. Pershing Elementary, become immune to the name calling and the word *nigger*, and met a handful of so-called middle-class blacks. I learned most of them merely lived in mediocre apartments near the white colonies. They dressed nicely, seemed okay, but talked more white than the white children. Immediately I, and most other project blacks, believed they tried to walk, talk, and breathe like white kids. "Get real, Scott. Gosh, Sue. Gee-whiz, Jeff." I don't see how they had time for anything else because they concentrated so hard on trying to mimic the white kids. Often, if I had not looked to see who was talking, I would have sworn it was one of those ultrawhite kids babbling—and not a black boy whose skin was more chocolate than mine. Some of them wouldn't have anything to do with us project blacks, either.

Like other project blacks, I never had time to concentrate on studies. My morale stayed low. My diet was terrible—when I had a diet. The lack of food probably caused more problems than I ever discovered. The last thing I wanted to think about was studying when I had a three-day-old hunger headache. I had no family support—my mother was too busy battling her own culture shock to assist me. And I never got proper rest in that oven unit. As every day went on, I slipped farther and farther behind the white kids, widening the already huge gap I would have to close. Every day I felt overwhelmed.

During my schooling at John J. Pershing, I was still evaluated all the time. Mrs. Nancy Raines, a white school counselor, would take me into her office and give me aptitude tests in math, reading, logic, and other subjects. Soon she tapped into some of the same signs the teachers at George Washington Carver had. My grasp of these skills was far advanced for my age, Mrs. Raines said, and she recommended me for advanced classes. Before long, I was taken out of "regular classes" and placed in the all-white, talented and gifted class, otherwise known as the TAG program.

My first day there, all the white children sat in a circle with the teacher and handed a box around. I was asked to join in, so

I took a seat. The object of the exercise was to guess what was in the box by using methods other than sight. Many kids had asked questions, but when the box was handed to me, I closed my eyes and shook the box several times. Then I asked the teacher if the object had plastic on it. She said yes, and one white kid said it was about time someone got a right answer. Later, a girl guessed that it was a plastic flower lying hidden in the box. For reasons unknown to me, that event really impresssed the white kids.

When news spread around the school that I was in TAG, I earned the admiration of some of my project peers. They would smile at me with pride gleaming in their eyes. I represented them, the children from the projects. I was their man in TAG, their man downtown, so to speak. And TAG helped to distract attention away from my smelly, dirty clothes.

My mother was extremely proud when she finally heard the good report. She had shared the news with her dope fiend friends, about how smart her baby boy was. The dope dealers had given me extra money and scolded my mother for not supporting the potential of her son. Junior and Sherrie weren't surprised. I had been doing Sherrie's high school homework and Junior had been consulting me on his middle-school work.

In the TAG classes, students were exposed to a wide curriculum: logic exercises, foreign languages, reasoning, and business management skills. In regular classes, a kid only learned basic reading and writing. On the days I came to school, I looked forward to TAG. I was mostly left alone and allowed to read. I enjoyed the challenges of trying, along with other students, to figure out a business budget, locate Italy on a world map, or say "Good morning" in French.

The teacher astonished all of us one day when she held up a book as thick as a dictionary and said she had read it last night. None of us could believe that she had read that book in so short a time. I had no idea this would become a common practice for me.

At Pershing, I had been missing school as much as I attended, because I was either ashamed of being dirty, was too hungry or too sick, or was required by my mother to miss school. Still, over the months I had become an eager student, wanting to participate in all the class activities. But I didn't even have pencil and paper. Though I had gotten a little praise from my mother, the children, and the dope dealers in the beginning, all of them went back to their respective routines. Furthermore, my happiness didn't last, because TAG didn't change the Hitler camp. I was eventually placed back in regular classes. I hated that.

Seeing my disappointment, Mrs. Raines kept me around for a short while. I even started writing a book. I would come into her office and longhand my story; then she would type it for me. It was about a young boy who sneaked out of his house on a rainy night to play tennis, when a spaceship caught and beamed him aboard.

One day in Mrs. Raines's office, when I was taking a make-up test, roaches ran from my book bag. Mrs. Raines smashed them hard with her hand, as if she had never seen one. The other students in the room laughed at me. My relationship with Mrs. Raines was never the same. Not that she rejected me. I was just too ashamed to have anything else to do with her. And I believed she felt my case was hopeless. So I stopped coming around.

Afterward, school became more unpleasant. For example, in the lunch room they made the paying students go through one line and the free lunch kids go through another. It was so humiliating. Mr. Holley, the PE teacher, called me into his office one day and made me show him my once white but now brown socks. He did the same with my underwear. He encouraged me to wash out my clothes by hand and to bathe myself, and he offered to take me to get a haircut. But I refused. Most of us boys wanted to keep our thick hair. And I wasn't concerned with bathing and cleaning clothes.

Attending school at Pershing offered me my first exposure to a wide variety of books. I believe my desire for understanding at that time got me into reading—since there were few human

sources. I read my history and reading books the first week of
school, from beginning to end. I would sit in class and, instead
of participating, read books: I read everything I could get my
hands on, even several encyclopedias. I even skipped recreation,
to read in the library or alone in the field. The reading wasn't
focused, but simply a random, indiscriminate process.

Over the spring of 1980, after my first year in the white school,
I began visiting the West Dallas Public Library to satisfy my new
love. Before, I didn't even know we had a library. I began to skip
school and read at the library all day, for ten and twelve hours,
sometimes until closing. I read books on hypnosis, psychic powers, and thinking, and encyclopedias to get information about
specific subjects. I read a lot of science fiction, too, Ursula K. Le
Guin, J.R.R. Tolkien. In addition, I read plenty of "how to"
books, on training dogs, camping, designing paper airplanes, or
whatever interested me that day. Books became my teacher and
my escape. I read voraciously, unmethodically, at the public
library for days and years.

Around the house, activity was changing again. Another man
was staying around more than usual. He would sit in our living
room after he had been upstairs with my mother and smoke his
tobacco pipe. If my mother let a man spend several nights, this
meant she had plans to keep him. I figured it was time to get to
know him after a week.

This one's name was Henry. He was tall, light-skinned, quiet,
and simple. In his thirties, he was content just to have a young
woman let him stay with her. Henry was also on heroin. But as
he stayed with us, I realized he wasn't so bad.

Early each morning Henry would walk across the long Hampton bridge to the truck docks, to load and unload the semis for
a small fee. With the money, he and my mother got high or
occasionally bought some lunch meat and bread or a chicken to
eat.

Henry took an interest in me and would advise me about putting my God-given intelligence to use. "Jerrold, you have a lot of sense. I hope you grow up and make something out of yourself." A lot of people would make this comment, but none of them ever said how to do it. And Henry was a bit of a coward to me. He wouldn't help Sherrie or me when we had to fight, wouldn't even come out of the house. Because he helped my mother supply her heroin, he became more important to her than we were: He ate before us, and we would receive a savage beating if she detected the slightest disrespect of him.

After school one evening, Henry introduced me to fishing. He took me down to the pond with two rod and reels and a bucket of worms he had dug up from his mother's backyard. We sat very close to the cattails, where he schooled me about fishing. First, he pointed at a long water moccasin that was relaxing in the cattails. "Don't disturb it," he said. Just beyond the cattails he cast the lines into the water. He propped them up in the air using a Y stick and twisted the reels until the lines were tight. We sat for a few minutes. I was told to watch the movement of the tip of the rod, which would signal a fish nibbling or nudging the bait. I sat with little interest, paying no attention to the rod I should have been watching. I heard Henry say, "There he goes." I turned around in time to see the rod bend almost to the water. As suddenly as it had tightened, the line slackened. "There are carps in this lake as long as a man's leg," Henry lectured. I went on to love the activity and to catch fish as big as Henry described, some so enormous we had to go into the water and drag them out by their gills.

Although I believe the fishing time was special for Henry and my mother, I stayed detached during our time together. As long as Henry or I cast the line, she would sit there and haul in the fish. Her skin had darkened from sitting in the sun all day. I believed my mom unconsciously used the activity to combat her drug habit, though it never worked.

But Henry eventually did something that made me dislike

him. He convinced my mother to sell drugs with him. They started selling for Nick*, Shortleg Lee's brother. Now my mother was a drug dealer again, and I knew it was only a matter of time before the gun-toting gangsters kicked down our door like they had done before, only now they would probably kill us. Because their drug habit came first, I knew things always went wrong when dope fiends dealt the dope, too.

Eventually my mother's new career brought more of her free-loading fiend friends around. They kept death near us. One evening I ran to the back door. As I jerked open the screen, this dope dealer who was visiting my mother kicked me hard between the legs, so hard that it made me urinate on myself. I flew backward through the air and hit the ground. I saw him reach for his revolver, then stop when he recognized me. When I walked back up to the door, he hit me in the face and told me never to run up and startle him.

I said, "Excuse me. I didn't know we were entertaining some panicky dope dealer. I thought I was allowed to run up to my back door." My mother just stood there and said nothing to the man for busting up her son. She probably was afraid to.

Along with oddballs like the panicky dealer were people like Big Mary. She came around more than the others. She weighed around three hundred pounds, with rolls of flesh on her huge arms and legs. She was clever, her every intention ill. With her big earrings, she reminded me of a fat voodoo woman. Big Mary always brought her skinny flunky husband with her when she came to our house, and the black-toothed jerk would go through our icebox and eat every bit of food we had left.

Always with a pleasant yet insidious undertone, Big Mary would shoot us her nettled smile. I hated how she slithered my name from her mouth like a lizard. "Jerrold, come talk to you Aunt Mary. Tell me what you momma's been doing." My mother was easy to manipulate, and the vulture Mary pecked away every bread crumb she could. She would encourage my mother to waste her welfare checks, always making sure she received her cut first.

She knew she was depriving us by doing this, but Big Mary didn't care. That vulture did it to her own kids, so what the hell, free bread crumbs.

However, one of my mother's friends, despite being as hooked on dope as the rest of them, did me a favor. She took me into the bathroom to make me bathe. I wasn't going to let her, but she won my confidence with her brisk but polite comments.

"Boy, I've seen many men before, so there's no reason for you to be ashamed." As I sat in our bathtub, she used a kitchen knife to scrape the dirt from my ankles. I avoided her eyes as I watched the water blacken with dirt. The woman told me not to be ashamed because it wasn't my fault.

"But don't let me see you let yourself go like this again, Jerrold," she said. She said I should learn to take care of myself and not depend on my mother. I never forgot her lesson, even after she stopped coming around.

When a kid had parents selling drugs, he did one of two things: moved with relatives or stayed away from the house as much as possible. Junior, Sherrie, and I had to take the second alternative. When the house was crowded with these noisy dope heads, when smoke, needles, and trash were everywhere, we would get the hell away. Sherrie would go to her boyfriend's grandmother. Junior would hop down to Big Mark's house. And I would linger with the older boys, would go to some pool or conversational gathering, or would play football in the wide field. Sometimes I would do just as Eric and I had done: sit on the money swings and watch the noisy people. At night I still watched the stars.

If stars were most visible in the late hours, my mother must have seen a lot of them. Her new career kept her out all night with Henry, among the black blackness. Sometimes she didn't come home. During these times, Sherrie began to take care of Junior and me. She made us come in the house, bathe, and lay out school clothes. When there was food, she made sure we ate, too. In a way, we all were growing closer, leaning more on each other for support. Even in the darkest hours, at our ages of nine, eleven, and thirteen, we were finding our inner strength, to help us deal with our daily tribulations.

But I never would have figured Junior could be brought from his privacy, his isolation, to defend Sherrie. It was a very late night, when my mother again was gone, that Sherrie crawled into our room. The trip from her room to ours certainly didn't require her to crawl. But the heavy black rapist on her back did. She managed to fall on Junior and me, waking us up. In my sleep I mumbled something about making the man wait in the living room until Momma returned. I had become so used to men being in our house that I thought his visit was just routine.

But when he made the three of us stand by the closet, I understood. We weren't nervous or frantic. We kept asking him what he wanted and telling him that our mother would be back soon. In response he kept telling Sherrie to come with him. Finally Junior bravely stepped forward. Junior, who had run from every bully in the projects, who hated violence like Gandhi, told the man that no matter what he did to us boys, he wasn't going to harm my sister.

Junior had a lot of undiscovered physical strength. He was very stocky and muscular, so he probably could have given the man a good battle. And Sherrie and I would have helped, probably would have hit the man in the head with a hammer or stabbed him with one of the kitchen knives. We were hard enough to do that.

Luckily, that wasn't necessary. When the rapist went to check things out at the front door, we put Sherrie through our bedroom window while shouting, "Run, run!" She sprinted to Mrs. Burnese's house, where she knocked on Mrs. Burnese's back door so hard that the glass at the top of the door broke. Mrs. Burnese's son, Charles, ran after the rapist with a pistol. But he already had vanished.

In the dark, I ran through the Deadman units I knew so well

to go call the police. They came a little late, about two hours later. We spent the rest of that day on Mrs. Burnese's living room floor and didn't see our mother until the next day.

Man, my family was buried under all this pressure. Things definitely were coming all the way apart. Even throughout that night at Mrs. Burnese's, as I sat up sleepless, I doubted we would ever make it, unless we found an Almighty force, maybe one who held the power of life and death in His hands.

5

SAVE ME, LORD

It had been almost two years in the gruesome projects since the man tried to rape my sister. I had gotten to know Mrs. Burnese, who was ancient in the projects, and her grandson, Sherrie's boyfriend, enough to visit them more often.

As I visited, I had heard Mrs. Burnese talk about her episodes with ghosts. Most adults in the projects claimed to have had an experience with one. She could tell the most terrifying stories. Always after nightfall, she would gather us children in her living room on the hard tile near the two couches. While we sat in a semicircle at her feet, she would bring the spirits alive.

Because her storytelling was so strong, it seemed as though the ghost would gather with us, would come from the dark pantry or from upstairs to listen to her tales. She seemed to be such a truthful woman, so she left everyone in fear. After each story, Mrs. Burnese, with her prunly wrinkled skin, so dark it looked burnt, and with her red, knowledgeable eyes and towering height, would warn us to respect the dead.

Her favorite story was about a man with fiery red eyes. "He was big, black, and cold," she said. She had seen him on a late trip to the bathroom one night. On her way back to bed, she looked downstairs, and there he stood. "Hey, whatcha doin' down there?" she had screamed. But he just stood there, blank and cold and without expression. She said she knew he wasn't anything living. Yelling, she ran and jumped into bed with her husband. He grabbed his pistol and ran downstairs, ignoring her objections.

"What could he do with a ghost?" she said. But his disbelief had forced him to investigate. Downstairs, he found the doors and windows secure, no sign of forced entry anywhere. "He must have come through the walls," said Mrs. Burnese. After hearing several of her stories, I stopped walking past the graveyard on my way to the shopping center.

Henry stayed around our house a few months after the rapist had come. On a night when dope money was hard to come by, he shot up a lot of the dope and fled with the proceeds from the rest. This upset my mother severely. She stayed restless and upset after his departure—but it was routine to us kids. She paced around the house, listened to old love songs on the radio, and stared yearningly out the window. She and Henry had become two dope fiends in love.

We all were terrified of the house after the rapists. Sherrie began spending most of her time with Teresa or Mrs. Burnese; Junior hung around more at Big Mark's house. I still visited the library, reading volumes of books. We all were just stagnating. We knew killers were going to come.

So when the candy man came instead, his arrival was a boon in disguise. This white man lived in a suburb to the west of Dallas. He would arrive each evening to recruit black boys for his illegal candy business. Drunk Tom, who was a wino with a year or two of college, told me to go with him. "You can feed your family," he had said. That was all I needed to hear.

Sitting in a van with seven other kids, I was taught a speech that claimed the job was a design to keep young boys off the streets and out of trouble by giving them a part-time job. Scott*, a cunning white man, also made sure I could count his money.

Scott was small: some of the older boys were twice his size. He tried to make up for this by talking sternly and barking orders, something we tolerated for the money. But toward the black adults in the projects he acted benevolent and concerned. Everybody saw through his act.

He would take about eight of us to a suburb, fill our carry boxes with candy, then make us work up and down a street, selling his candy. As soon as we sold out, he would pick us up, reload the boxes, and take us to another street.

I recited his speech at every door: "Hello, sir. My name is Jerrold Ladd. I'm with the Junior Careers of Texas. This job is designed to keep us black boys off the streets and out of trouble." *It also makes us do illegal work because my boss is not licensed, doesn't pay taxes on the money, and works us for under one dollar an hour. We'll soon have criminal records. He's making a bundle, too.*

Some of the white people were sympathetic, but a lot of them were cruel. They slammed doors in our faces, and others called the police on us. The police busted us in one city, took mug shots and fingerprints. They dragged Scott downtown, too; but, after these incidents, he would just move to another city, until he was busted again. The white people sicced their dogs on us. One of them had bitten a young boy real bad. Scott did nothing.

Scott sometimes took us to his pleasant apartment, where his wife and son lived with him. He would do his books and other paperwork. He also would worship his scroll, a piece of paper in a box that he kneeled and prayed to for money and riches. He invited us to see the ritual one day. While down there on his knees, he chanted strange words in his off-key voice for about five minutes.

On another day, his wife asked me to stay home with her while Scott and the others went to the candy warehouse. I guess he thought she had plans to, say, make me take out the trash or a similar service. But she wanted something else.

She was a sweet, blonde-haired woman. As soon as Scott and the crew left, she put on a gown and we sat on the couch. She wasn't wearing a bra, and her blue panties were showing.

"Jerrold, you seem like a real special boy, different from the rest. I like the way you ask questions and keep quiet."

That woman really wanted to give me something for being special. She propped her legs up on the couch and opened them up on purpose. "Have you ever been with a woman, Jerrold?"

"No, I haven't."

"Do you want to try it, then, Jerrold? It's a wonderful experience."

Up to this point in my life, no concept of sex ever had entered my mind. My experience with Gloria had been far from sexual. So I just sat there, scared, saying nothing. After I didn't respond, Scott's wife changed her clothes and went on about her chores. She never asked me not to tell or anything, as though she didn't care if Scott knew or not.

When I told them later, all my friends who also worked for Scott laughed at me because I refused to go to bed with his wife. Surprisingly, they all claimed to have known what she wanted when she asked me to stay. They all said they would have done it.

By 1982 the candy man came less, then stopped coming altogether. I sat in my room one evening soon after. Right outside, an eerie, empty project unit reflected sunlight from its broken windows. Glass and trash, more than usual, littered the barren ground close by. Unusual sounds were coming from outside. I looked out my front door, trying to locate the amplified voice I was hearing bouncing off the project buildings. The voice was full of energy and shouted strange words. Excitement, unlike anything I previously had heard in the projects, was close. What was causing all the noise? I walked toward the voices onto Fishtrap Street to find out.

On a small patch of dirt in a resident's yard, a small group of people had gathered. Their faces were dry, stern, and serious. The women were wearing dresses, the men suits and neckties. They all held tambourines, which they patted against their hands while they stomped their feet to the rhythm. A lady held a microphone and sang: "Watcha gonna do, whatcha gonna do when the world's on fire?"

We gathered around to observe the singing and clapping. I remembered visiting several churches when we had lived somewhere with my father, but not since moving into Hades. And these people, they were not confined in a church but had brought their passion right outdoors, smack in the middle of the projects. As I watched them, I was glad that the dope dealers were being tolerant.

After the healthy woman finished singing, an elderly, set-faced man stepped forward to speak: "The Lord can bring ah change in your life. If you're hungry and worried, if you have bills to pay, if you're on drugs, whatevah the problem, the Lord can make a change." This elderly man spellbound me when he went on and talked about the God Who loved me and could make my life happy. He said that Jesus had died on the cross for my sins, and if I accepted Him into my life, I would be saved. I felt hurt and wanted this God to help me and my family. When he asked if anyone wanted to try Jesus, through the laughter of spectators, I nervously stepped forward. I was led off by a woman.

This woman, who acted like she had been through this ritual a thousand times, said, "Close your eyes, young man, and repeat after me." She prayed: "Lord, I believe that Jesus died for my sins, and I want to accept Him as my personal savior." I repeated every word. Others who had walked forward with me were being lectured in the background, as I was.

"Ask the Lord to save you."

I said, "Lord, save me."

She shouted in my ear, "Save me, Lord."

"Save me, Lord," I said.

"Ask the Lord to save you."

"Save me, Lord."

"Now thank Him."

"Thank you, Lord."

By then she was hyped and spitting in my ear. Some of the group members were making eerie ghost sounds. I opened my eyes and saw the fat singer bent forward, arms outstretched, screaming.

The intensity slowly let up. I was asked my name and told that I was now cleaned and saved. I now needed to come to the church to learn and grow. The arrangements were made. I walked back home, telling no one about my new secret.

The next Sunday I walked to church, without telling anyone where I was going. I had on my usual disgusting clothes. The church was fifteen minutes away, behind the redneck store. When I got there, everyone else was just arriving. The lady who had performed the ceremonial prayer introduced me on the church porch as Brother Ladd. The church had the same red bricks like the projects, but it was trimmed in white and had a small steeple at the top. Since we all were early, we went inside to take our seats among the wooden church benches.

I sat on the very first row and watched about fifty members file into the church. They looked like average project citizens: old men, fat gossipy women, children, and young couples. I was really nervous, yet curious to see how things worked in the church. Before long, the elders took their seats in the honorable-looking chairs at the front, and the service started. A young lady in her twenties stood before a microphone, and several people walked to the three entrances of the church and stood, like sentries. The young woman called on people to testify, and they told how God had blessed them with money for things like rent, a car part, and food.

Next, the woman on the tallest chair stepped forward. She was the leader of the church.

I didn't pay much attention to the pastor's message. I was watching the church members. They wailed, jumped, screamed, kicked, hollered, and threw their bodies around like they were possessed. They made eerie sounds that reminded me of Mrs. Burnese's spirits. Meanwhile, musicians were banging away on the organ, piano, and drums, enticing the people to jump higher and scream louder. It seemed as though the whole church were bouncing: pulpit, benches, and members.

After they handed around the offering tray two or three times, the service was over. Everyone left full of energy.

I soon learned how to pray, all about sin, living holy, the end of the world, and the crucifixion of Jesus Christ. I was told that God loved me and did not want to see me suffering, hungry, and deprived. Without hesitation, I trusted God. I went to the church every time they had service, maybe five or six times a week. Meanwhile, my mother began respecting my religious devotion, even though I was just twelve and still figuring out exactly what it was. She encouraged me to keep going to church. Word soon spread around my project block that I was saved.

Around the neighborhood, people were just about equally divided on how they viewed church. The younger generation had little interest in the strict, holy lifestyle; they often laughed at any young person claiming to be saved. The older generation, on the other hand, had a deep fear of hell and eternal damnation, the only thing I saw that made them go to church. Most thought it was their ticket to a better life someday, although many still did not attend a church. Regardless, I blocked out everything except my awe and interest in God.

Some Sunday mornings, after the congregation had departed, I sat on the church porch. I would wait there until the evening service began. I always sat on the first row, listening to every word that woman said about the wonderful God Who loved us all. For several months I watched the pattern of the church.

I soon learned that half the congregation came to worship; the other half came because parents or others dragged them there. There were a lot of cliques, too: "special-interest groups." The housewives would band together to talk about foolishness, such as how someone dressed, who was a hypocrite, or who didn't have nice clothes. The "unsaved," younger members came to lust after each other. People got married all the time, to get around the sin of fornication. As soon as a new man or woman joined, established church members who were interested in him or her would demonstrate this by claiming their "future spouse" during testimony service. "I know the Lord sent her to me," an interested man would say while looking at the attractive woman he knew so little about.

The so-called saved members did nothing but read the Bible, jump, moan, scream, cry, and beg God to help them pay the rent or put some crumbs on their dinner table. Nothing significant ever happened for them. Occasionally someone would land a minimum-wage job or hustle up a few hundred dollars through hard work—like mowing lawns or painting. Then he would testify about this at church, as if he had just been given a million dollars. In response, the church would rock and roll.

The pastor kept fear in all of us by preaching on eternity in hell. That was her most common sermon. She blatantly taught contradictory information. For example, she said that we would inherit our reward in heaven but should be tolerant of being poor now. At the same time, she taught that God would give more to his own saved children on earth than he would to the unsaved and the wicked. In effect, if you were saved, you should expect to live above the standard of the unsaved, the sinner.

But dope dealers, alcoholics, my sweet friend who didn't eat pork, and every white person I knew who didn't respect the holy religion lived better than these saved people. The whites had much more than anybody, more than the church members who were doing all they could to adhere to the holy lifestyle, giving all their money to the church while living in their shacks, filth, and trash—these good people, who were trying to live spotless to enter the Pearly Gates, the pie in the sky. They surely were living according to the pastor's gospel and surely were not reaping the benefits. On the other hand, those who had no regard for the church were in paradise.

But I soon became swallowed up in the same process. I shouted and testified every time the pace increased, allowing the mood of the atmosphere to take me. My feet stomped, my voice wailed. I became well trained in the biblical Scripture and the knowledge the pastor taught about God. I started witnessing to other people the way the lady had witnessed to me. I was happy to know I could have a good normal life, never hungry, always happy.

I only had to die before I received it.

After a few months of this, I prepared for my biggest challenge. I turned my faith toward my house. God was going to take my mother off drugs. I knew He would do it, possessed no doubt. I discussed my plans with one of the men who sat on the honorable chairs. He was quiet, didn't holler like the others when he preached. I admired him more than I did the other ministers. Whenever he was asked to give a sermon, I listened extra carefully. But the rest of the congregation would sit bored to death, since there wasn't any screaming, jumping, and shouting going on.

One day after Sunday service I told the quiet minister I was having problems at home; my mother was on drugs, we were poor, didn't eat half the time. I told him we wanted a better life. He told me to believe in God.

That evening, when I arrived home, I put my plan to action. The house was in its usual dirty, sticky, and scorch hot condition. Sherrie was away, and Junior was playing in our room. I was nervous and knew I had to act fast. If she caught me, she would surely bust me up. I ran water in the face bowl, acting as if I were busy in the bathroom. After looking down the stairway several times, watching for her, I hurried into her room and looked through the several dresser drawers. There they lay, several syringes and a couple of cigarettes wrapped neatly in a plastic bag.

I was pumped with faith, awe, and fear as I held the package in my hand. I took the stuff to the Dumpster on the corner, as far away as possible.

Later that night, she shuffled home. She wasn't in the room five minutes before she tore into the hallway, on fire!

"Jerrold, Junior, who done been in my room, gaddammit? I told you motherfuckers not to let nobody in here when I'm gone. Go find Sherrie and tell her I said to bring her tail home right now. I'm sick of this."

I walked up to her room door, knocked, and went inside. I boldly told her what I had done. I told her that God loved and wanted to help us. Then I lowered my head and waited for her wrath and fire. But my words disturbed her. She just stood there looking twisted, just seething with anger, but she didn't let loose her flurry of hooks and uppercuts. As I have mentioned, the older generation had a deep fear of God. I think she was afraid of the consequences of charging one of His humble believers.

Instead, she told me to get the hell out and shut the door. I did what she asked; but instead of leaving, I sat at the top of the stairs by her room door. I stayed there several hours, waiting for her to come out again. She eventually came out and took a seat beside me. I told her that we could do better, that God was making me happy, and that He wanted to do the same thing for her. "Yeah, baby, I know," she said. After our talk, we decided that our family would go to church together, the next Sunday.

So my mother, sister, brother, and I went to church. When the pastor asked who wanted to be saved, they went to the altar. They each went through the ritual, and my mother wailed like a seasoned pro. I felt ashamed as she yelped, screamed, and spoke in the same garbled language the church people had forced me to use—the ministers had said unless I spoke in a strange tongue, I didn't have the Holy Ghost.

After we arrived home that evening, I noticed a worried look in my mother's eyes. As strong as her desire was, she was still helpless. We talked for a couple of hours. I finally made her tell me what was bothering her.

She would have to face Nick, Shortleg Lee's brother, who had recently returned from out of town. She thought he would kill her. Standing at the front door, not wanting to go, she wore her usual grimace of worry. I asked her if she wanted me to go talk to him. But she thought it best if she explained the circumstances to him. "No, baby, let Mama go and do this. You just stay here and watch the house. I'll be all right."

As I watched her walk out the door and over to Nick's house, I wondered if I would ever see her again. I started after her several times, wondering if I could help, if Nick would respect my religious zeal, my weapons of faith. But I didn't go. Nick had machine guns.

An hour later, she returned happily. He had forgiven her, said he wouldn't kill her. Now we could go on with our lives. Now we could get the happiness that we saved people were due. But that was not to be the case for us or anyone I can recall who went to any black church.

No matter how hard we prayed, stomped, and waited, few things changed. Occasionally someone would hand me a thrift pair of pants or a shirt. Some members would get a car part or some old clothes, but nothing more. The church was teaching us how to remain in the ghettos, shacks, and slums and beg every day for the decency that we should have been striving to get. No emphasis was placed on self-improvement, education, self-reliance, better jobs, better housing, or extensive study of our religious beliefs. It was just shut up and wait to die. And while you're waiting, stay worried and deprived. And put your last pennies in the offering bucket.

Eventually my brother was the first to stop attending the church; Sherrie would remain in church for a little longer but she stopped attending, too. No matter how hard my mother tried, her peace of mind came only from the heroin. I kept attending the services for a while, until I could no longer ignore the destruction I saw. People were going through the church like it had revolving doors. Dozens of eager new faces, families, and single mothers dragging hungry babies were popping up each Sunday. Looking for hope, a way out, some relief. They all stomped, wailed, cried, moaned, and waited. Some new members stayed and joined one of the "special-interest groups." Others would get that special car part or husband. But all of them always emptied their pockets.

I also noticed how everyone became naturally disturbed when the sermon hinted around the color of the son of God and the origins of the religion. The leaders' knowledge of the religion was limited. And they could never answer the question of whether it was truly ours.

Among the gossip, grief, hunger, and sorrow, my church activities diminished. I soon left, unannounced, never to return. We had entered the revolving church doors depressed and nowhere. We came out more depressed and worse than nowhere.

6

DO IT FOR MOMMA

To avoid the projects, I would explore the area surrounding where we lived in west Dallas. I found places like Hooky Hill, the shack houses, and nearby public pools, which the older boys and I would sneak into at night. I stayed out late. The church had dealt a tremendous blow to my already fragile hope. And it also had pushed my mother over the edge, caused her to abuse her children as never before. After we had left the church, I really knew we would always be in these projects, suffering.

With Henry gone, the rotating fathers returned. My mom stopped selling drugs but again took up her drug routine, this time with renewed desperation. She went back to her solace from reality. The kinder, gentler mother we had experienced for a few weeks was gone. She was replaced by a monster who gave more beatings, did more screaming, and saw more men. The waves of cigarette smoke, people, and dope kept our house like a cesspool.

One evening my mother called me into her bedroom. "Go borrow Momma a cigarette," she said. Without looking at her, I walked away. At least it gave me a reason to get out of the house. I headed to the corner where the dope dealers worked, where I had learned that I could find plenty of smokers. One-arm Nathan sat underneath a tree, shading himself from the late sun. Another man stood nearby, puffing on a cigarette. I walked up to him.

"My momma wants to know if she can borrow a cigarette," I said.

Several seconds passed before the man showed any sign he had heard me. He suddenly looked down. "What did you say?"

"My mom wants a cigarette."

Without looking at me, he talked toward the heavens, as if he were too embarrassed to face the child he was about to corrupt: "I know where we can get a lot of money and you can buy your momma all the cigarettes you want." The man looked at me for the first time. He was coming down from a hard high. His eyes were red; his nose was running. He told me he knew where some foreigners lived who were out of town and who had a lot of money. "If you help me carry their belongings to my car," he said, "I'll give you some money." Though nervous and scared, and only twelve, I went with him. The fiend was desperate for a fix. I was desperate for everything.

Several blocks away we arrived at the back of a unit. The sun had just set, and the dark darkness was coming. He picked up a brick near the apartment and shattered the glass. Uncautiously we walked over to the only thing of value in the unfurnished apartment, a floor-model TV. We picked up the TV and carried it to a nearby car.

Nervously he shouted through the car window at someone sitting inside: "Wake your ass up, man." The man came quickly from his sleep, as if he had been waiting for the moment. I leaned against the car, trying to pretend I wasn't scared. But I was shaking like a wet puppy. The man got out of the car and helped his partner put the TV in the trunk. They got into the front seat. Then I slipped into the backseat at his bidding, and we drove away.

After two turns we pulled into a parking lot on Fishtrap near my unit. Most of the streetlights were out, and as usual, the projects were under a black night. People were standing around like so many fading shadows. The man and I entered an abandoned unit, one that was a market for fiends and dealers. The driver waited for us.

"I'm gonna whoop your ass," said a voice from the darkness. My mother came forward and grabbed me by my shirt. She was mad as hell, seeing that her son was following in her footsteps. She lost the composure that experienced women like her kept and for several seconds turned into a concerned mother. But my quick-thinking partner told her that he had just met me walking up the street and had offered me money to help him carry the TV. Relieved, my mother sent me home after telling me she would bring my money. As I walked home, I knew I would never see any of it.

My mother did not come back that night, and my sister came home late. This was every man for himself now, so I wasn't concerned. The next morning I dressed and went into the kitchen to make a ketchup sandwich, but the ketchup was all gone. All the food was gone. Without hesitating, I began the walk to the shopping center, being sure to take the lake route to avoid Three Finger Willie and Syrup Head. When I got there, I boldly walked into the store, stuck a bag of rice in my pants, and walked straight out. And over the next few weeks, when my hunger would not let me rest, I stole again and again.

To steal food was no real challenge. I knew how the managers looked. The stores had no cameras, no mirrors. I would wait until a section was free of customers, then stuff the can or the bag in my jacket or crotch. I didn't really care. If I had been spotted, I would have run circles around the white managers and darted out the door.

After stealing food became habitual, it was on to the toy store next to Tom Thumb. The personnel there were more watchful. Even so, I once tried to walk out with a big toy truck. I was caught at the door. Police officers took me home, where my mother promised a whooping, one I would never get.

Junior was back on his all-day buggy routines. Sherrie stayed away from the house with her boyfriend, Junebug, who lived north of the projects in Richardson. She was spending nights at his house while telling my mother she was at his grandmother's. Our mother stayed locked away in her room. My stealing was increasing, and the stakes were becoming higher. Everyone was going down a bad road. We became silent, hardly speaking to each other.

We worked harder: "Borrow Momma a cigarette, steal Momma some aspirin, go buy Momma a nerve pill." She stayed angry and had more seizures and fits than usual. She would fly from her room and whoop us with the first thing in sight. At night the house seemed baneful, despair seemed bottomless. Behind her room door, my mother would cry and wail like she was possessed. Things got so bad that people in the projects were predicting my mother would soon be murdered or go insane, and that the state people would come and get us. But she made a final attempt to preserve her family. She jumped out of her trance. God knows where she found the strength.

On that day, she had just come from using a neighbor's phone and into the kitchen where my sister, brother, and I were. "Go and pack some clothes," she told us as she hurried up the stairs.

"Momma, where are we going?" I asked.

"We're going to spend the summer with Sister Hill*."

"Who is Sister Hill?"

"Jerrold, she's someone I used to go to church with. Now quit bugging me, and go pack some clothes." She disappeared up the stairs.

An hour later, we had locked the house up and were waiting on the porch. An elderly man pulled his church van into the

Fishtrap parking lot and honked his car horn. My brother and I hurried to the church bus to avoid being seen by our friends. We were ashamed of having this church man coming to get us. But a smile flashed across my mother's face.

After a fifteen-minute drive, we arrived at the home of Sister Hill. She was a middle-aged woman who lived alone. Her four children were grown and didn't live there. Her poor black neighborhood was made up of houses and apartment complexes and located on Dixon Circle, where a lot of filth and crime took place. She never had visitors, and the house stayed hot. But she was nice, baked all kinds of goodies, and wailed like the people at the church.

The first few weeks, she and my mother sat around all day reading the Bible. My sister left to stay with a friend. The stress on my brother and me eased. We would stay in the apartment all day, watching the new woman make candy apples, or would go outside to catch fireflies in the surrounding woods. Once we had exhausted ourselves outdoors, we would lie and sweat on the couches. It was the same routine for the first month: play, sweat, and sleep. And then Sister Hill's lusty niece came around.

Jackie's* skin was fair and silky. Only sixteen, she had the kind of body that attracted men. Her eyes always glistened with a curiosity for what the world and men held for her. For excitement, she would visit the young boys in the apartment complex. The minute her mom dropped her off, she would shoot out the door and not return until nightfall. Jackie would sleep in one of the bedrooms, even though the house stayed cooler in the living room. She usually ignored my brother and me, until one day she asked my mother if I could walk her to the store.

Jackie and I worked our way through the complex to a street that led to the neighborhood grocery. Everyone was outside making noise—families, kids, wine heads, street peddlers. Though the sun had begun to set, it was still hot.

"Jerrold, what did you do every day at your house?" she asked as we walked to the store.

"I mostly kept to myself."

"Did you have a girlfriend?"

"No."

"Have you ever had a girl before?"

"Yeah."

"Who?"

I lied. "I've had a whole lot of girls."

Jackie smiled. "Quit lying, boy. You haven't had sex."

Several girls walked past us. They exchanged frowns with Jackie. She dropped the conversation and asked me if I wanted anything from the store. but on the way back she started again.

"I'm gonna see what you're all about tonight."

"What do you mean?" I asked, already knowing exactly what she meant.

"I'm gonna be the first to have you."

We ate a small dinner, then got ready for bed. Later that night, Jackie began to work her womanly magic, fulfilling her prediction. She decided to sleep in the living room. Since there were only two couches, she would have to share a couch with someone. She chose the one I slept on, the one close to the window. Sister Hill and my mother, after staying in the hot apartment all day, dozed quickly. My brother soon joined them.

Jackie squeezed her slim body onto the couch and snuggled herself close to my private parts. Then, after a while, she began to move back and forth. Not wanting to seem soft, I moved along with her. She moved and moved, as if she were being satisfied.

She then etched words into my memory that I have never forgotten, that I would hear again from another who would also take advantage of a child. "Jerrold, I know you can do it good. I'm gonna go back in the room. You wait awhile, then come back there with me." Before rising, she said, "Do it for me, baby." I watched her walk to the back room. After her warm words, which made something deep inside me respond, I followed her into the room and shut the door behind me.

* * *

When that summer came to an end in 1984, we returned to our old unit, where the tension still dwelled. Things quickly went back to normal—washing sinks full of pots and pans, cleaning up bathrooms, mopping tile floors. My mom made us do everything. I began to think we were slaves. She would send us to a neighbor's house to buy her pain pills for a dollar fifty each. If the neighbor was out, we were told to walk miles to other places, even if it was three o'clock in the morning. She started smoking more cigarettes. And we were sent to buy or steal them. I hated it, hated the cigarette smoke, hated the slave work. But the cool words "Do it for Momma" did me in every time. Kindness was so rare.

"Bring Momma's house shoes, wash out Momma's panties." And I hardly ever objected, because if I did, I would receive one of those terrible beatings with an extension cord or get slapped across the face. One time, before one of her blows landed, I darted out the door and called her a bitch. I climbed a tree until I thought the action had cooled down. Wash out Momma's panties, do this for Momma, do that for Momma. My brother and I continued to leave the house early so we wouldn't have to slave for Momma all day.

Then it finally happened. One day in autumn, the mailman delivered the notice that we had thirty days to vacate our project unit. We had no money. The gorilla workers would soon come. During that time, my mother stayed depressed and finally broke.

Two days later she screamed my name. Pain was in her voice: "Jerrold!"

"Yes, ma'am," I responded, while hurrying up the stairs.

I came into the bathroom, where she sat on the toilet. Her face was twisted worry. A stocking was tied around her arm. She brought a syringe up to it and said, "Jerrold, I'm too nervous to hit myself. I'll put the needle to my arm. All you'll have to do is squeeze it."

73

I was in a trance. I quietly came into the bathroom and shut the door behind me. She placed my hand on the needle with her nervous, shaking hand and said, "Do it for Momma." A little kid, I understood her torment, her complete dependence. I held her shaking arm still while squeezing the clear liquid into her. I did it for Momma.

7

STRUGGLE

Days after the incident with my mother, Junior was sent to the store for aspirin again. My mother sent him with a fifty-dollar bill given to her by a stranger. He returned promptly, as usual, and gave her the aspirin and change. She disappeared. A half hour later, a tall, angry man came by looking for her. He asked Junior, who was standing in our backyard, for the money. Surprised, Junior told him he had given our mother the change. "She told me you never gave it to her," the man said. Our mother had taken this man's money and left him expecting something in return.

He was angry, angry enough that he hit my gentle brother across the face. Junior cried out as he staggered back against the wire clothesline. Sherrie, who had been looking from our back door, dashed past the man, who grabbed for her, and ran next door to the bootleg to call the police. The man stood in the bootleg door, screaming and cursing at the top of his lungs. I stood peering around the side of the project building with Little Mark.

As we watched, our fight-or-flight mechanism clicked. Which one would we choose to do, aid Junior or run like cheetahs? Sudden fear came over Mark. He dashed for his house. I decided to run also and darted through the Deadman units. I felt guilty for leaving my brother and angry because I was too skinny to do anything. But too many people had been killed by men like that. Besides, I had decided this was my last run. I headed to a friend's house to call the police. I would send them for Junior. But I was never going back.

Alone in an empty Deadman unit after making the call, I played until the sunset. Never in there after dark, I headed to the redneck store. For the first night, I planned to stay awake and roam the streets, watching all the depressed, noisy people.

But as I played a video game in the store with a feeling of dread, a man tapped on my shoulder. I spun around in a whirl of fear and saw a short, smiling black man. He was my uncle James, my mother's brother. "She said I would find you here," he said. He turned and walked out the store. Without question, I followed. As soon as we stepped through the door, a hard rain began to fall.

In the car on the stormy highway I talked with my sister, who had called our uncle, then showed him where to find me. She said the police, who she had called also, came hours later. Our mother never came back. But Junior was safe at our uncle James's house.

Since my mother had not stayed in contact with her three brothers and four sisters across town, Uncle James was unaware of his sister's life. We let him know how bad things had gotten. He shook his head in disbelief. Later he postponed conversations for the night, and after we ate a small meal, everyone went to bed.

Plans were made the next day. My sister was sent to my aunt

Cheryl's house. Junior and I remained with my uncle James. In a few days, he had moved our clothes and furniture from the Hitler camp. And we began to settle down.

James lived in East Ledbetter Apartments on Ledbetter, one of many apartment complexes scattered throughout Oak Cliff. The complexes were a grade above the project units, slightly larger, and had central air and heat.

A shopping center, barbecue shacks, and other restaurants were located at the busy intersection of Ledbetter and Bonnie View, just before the school. Most everyone around there, it seemed, tended to his own business.

My uncle James was the oldest of the boys, maybe three years behind my mother, the oldest of her family. He had shared the same family environment as my mother and had settled into hard, unrewarding labor to feed and clothe his family—although this clearly was not his ambition or the extent of his potential. He had a job doing office cleaning. He didn't smoke, drink, or do drugs. And he seemed to care about us. He had married in his early twenties but was divorced and the possessor of his three young children, two girls and a small boy. He had since remarried.

The noise and violence was less in Oak Cliff. It seemed a vast colony of minimum-wage workers, and I realized I finally had moved up to the minimum-wage group. I hoped my sturdy uncle would adopt me. But, at the same time, I wanted my mother to be here also. She could do better away from the projects.

Junior stayed for only a short time with Uncle James, then was sent to live with another aunt close by. I grew closer to my three cousins, all preschoolers, often riding them on the back of their bike in the scarcely populated apartments, the way Bad Baby had done for me in the projects. We played nonsense kid games all the time. Or watched TV!

In the near distance, the neighborhood had a small middle and high school, surrounded by better-quality housing than the ones near Robin Village. After several weeks passed, I enrolled into

James Bowie Elementary and found a white candy man in Oak Cliff. I quickly joined his sales team, again selling candy in the white neighborhoods after school and on weekends.

I only stayed in the all-black elementary school for several months, but I still liked it more than going to white schools. It felt right being with people who looked, acted, and thought like me. There was no constant humiliation, most everybody ate free lunches, and I made a lot of friends, something I never did at Pershing. I became more talkative at school, learned to play games, shoot marbles, talk about girls, and clown around with other black boys. Eventually I would begin to feel relief in the mornings, on the way to school, and pressure in the evenings.

At first I hardly missed my mother, but later I wondered how she was doing, wanted to see her in person. I had become very quiet and secretive about my feelings and thoughts. Despite this, I asked my uncle one evening about my mother's whereabouts. He told me he had found and encouraged her to admit herself into a drug rehabilitation center. We would go see her soon, he said.

If she does well, we even would be reunited with her.

In preparation for our reunion, I began to save the money from my candy sells. Each night I would give my uncle the eight, eleven or thirteen dollars I had earned. He promised he would put it away for me. Every night I also kept accurate figures on the money in a small notepad. In a few weeks I had earned sixty-seven dollars.

Meanwhile I found the complex where Junior lived, following my uncle's direction. My aunt Felisa, a real short lady, had four children and was not married. Although she didn't work, she tried to share what she had with Junior.

Junior was doing okay. He missed our mother more than I and was taking the change hard. He didn't have much to do since all his friends were gone, and he thought the future looked bleak. So I spent more time around there with him, trying to cheer him up. Then my own problems flared up.

On the day I was supposed to visit my mother, my uncle called me into his room. His usual solid demeanor was replaced by a look similar to my mother's twisted worry. "Jerrold, I have some bad news to confess to you." I just sat quietly. "All the money you had been giving me I spent on food to feed us."

I was outraged. "I want my money, I was saving that for my mother."

His wife intervened. "We're sorry we didn't tell you, but everyone had to eat. You have been helping to feed us," she said.

No explanation would do. He had no right to spend my money without my permission. I had planned to help my family rebuild. I wanted to show my mother that I could help. But I entered the car on my way to see her with empty pockets and with broken trust.

We drove only a few minutes, so the rehab must have been in another part of Oak Cliff. The two-story center was a remodeled, old wooden house. We pulled into the driveway. Inside, my mother sat in the living room area, watching TV with other addicts. Somebody escorted her and us to a private part of the place. She had gained weight, and her once fair, clear skin had been restored. Neither of us had anything to say. We just sat there going through the formalities. I was too upset at my uncle James. She was probably tired of being there. After James and his wife left, I told her what they had done with my money. She told me not to worry. But, obviously, she was worried and anxious to leave.

Back in East Ledbetter, I began to see things differently. What first had seemed like some real success for my uncle turned out to be nothing. James had depended on my modest earnings to help hold his family together, income I knew would not last long; white candy men spent only so much time in one area. James's needs answered many questions for me, mainly that he could barely support his own family. And even though he had boldly retrieved us, he was just as stricken as my mother. Taken together, these observations meant only one thing: I was a burden to him.

However, before I could pull him down completely, my mother was released. Before a month passed, she found her another man, who rented an apartment in a small, Hispanic part of Oak Cliff. I don't know if she came to get Junior and me because she wanted to or was legally obligated. She wasn't looking too happy to see us, two kids who were unwanted expenses. She wouldn't have to worry with my sister, who remained with our aunt.

On the rainy evening we departed, her eyes were sunk and crossed. She was high, which didn't surprise me. Junior and I walked back and forth to Uncle James's car, loading our few belongings, while trying to stay dry. It was raining as though Noah had come from the dead and resurrected the great rains.

I quickly saw that my mother was not affected by the drug treatment, which I had learned little about. But I believed it was not medical treatment, just a bunch of counseling by a lot of people who knew nothing about the forces that drove people like my mother to drugs. Once free, she used dope more vigorously. The treatment seemed only to have irritated her.

For the next two years, Junior, my mother, and I dotted the Oak Cliff area of Dallas, moving every few months. We first moved into a duplex house in another part of Oak Cliff on Lancaster Street, a Mexican neighborhood. Trash and other litter were left far too long on the street curbs and alleys, because the city trucks used an erratic schedule in this community. Most of these people spoke broken English and were buried under layer after layer of odds, like us. The state vans would come and the state men would storm the Mexicans' houses, seeking illegal aliens.

Often and throughout the day, dozens of Mexicans drank beer and listened to Spanish songs from portable radios. Among the hundreds of Mexican families were a handful of black families. Here, too, everyone minded his own business.

My mother had a new boyfriend, Sam*, who reminded me of

Henry, in that he was kind and worked but had a serious drug habit. He had grown up in the west Dallas housing projects, where his mother still lived. A small man, perhaps 160 pounds, he consumed daily more alcohol than the amount of water both Junior and I drank daily. He, like many others, was content just to share the same house with my lovely, gorgeous mother, regardless of the demands.

While living in the lime-painted duplex on Lancaster, which had one bedroom, Junior and I slept on the living room floor without blankets, where we vomited and experienced diarrhea because of our hunger. My mother cared nothing for food and quickly lost the weight she had gained. She had an unspoken rule: All money except for rent, in some instances, goes for my drugs. Sometimes we didn't have electricity or water. Sam complied with her rules, as if he were her servant, even if this meant he himself went hungry. But my mother, regardless, stayed fed and full, from dope.

Driven by the hunger, Junior and I sought work again. We roamed up and down Jefferson Boulevard, a mile-long street full of merchant shops, asking for work. Junior, sixteen, was hired at a DAV thrift store. But I, only fifteen, still did not meet the legal age requirement for work.

So I stole food from the convenience store near our house. I met an Indian, Co-Chief, who had a key to video games, one day when we were stealing on the same aisle. After we became friends, we burglarized several games, gaining sixty dollars in quarters each. But the merchants caught on, so we had to diversify. Since neither of us attended school, we would get together early each morning to find something to pass the time. Co-Chief taught me several neat tricks about small-time thievery. To get some pocket change, we burglarized the newspaper machines. Co-Chief would take a clothes wire and stick putty on the end of it. He would put a quarter into a paper machine to open the door. This exposed the slot in which the quarters fell. He then would stick his clothes wire into the hole and fish out quarters. Once I learned how, either he or I would stand watch for the police while the other fished out quarters.

In the back of his house, we would bang and sand nickels into the shape of quarters. We used the tokens to buy sodas and snacks from vending machines and also to play video games.

Another trick we developed to play free video games required a quarter, some Scotch tape, and a piece of thread. The thread would be taped to the center of the quarter, so that it would balance vertically if you let it dangle from the end of the thread. We would then lower the quarter into the video game. When a quarter passes a certain point inside a video game, it triggers a switch that gives the customer credit for that quarter—if you drop three quarters into a game, the game will award you three credits. Once our rigged quarter touched the credit device, we would pull it gently, back and forth, until we had one hundred or so credits.

Co-Chief also introduced me to Mary, an old white lady in the area. She lived in a brick house where vines grew wildly. Her backyard was fenced and her front porch had several old couches. The woman was clearly over seventy and lived with her ancient mother. Mary bought almost anything, old coffee makers, tires, dogs, and dishes. Co-Chief and I would find someone's valu-able—at least valuable to us—and sell it to her. I even stole—or caught—dogs and was able to get ten or twenty bucks. Wrin-kled Mary would barely open her front door, looking ghostly white and smelling old, and reach out with her spotty crumbling hand. Sometimes she would talk in her trembling voice. "I don't think it's worth what you're asking." And she always kept one hand behind the door when she handed me the money, as though she held an ax or something. The money, just about every time, went on food or was given to my mother.

After a few months, we moved into another apartment complex down the street. Mildewed, it had a broken frame, old wood, compact rooms. We stayed only two weeks. My mother took the rent money—and pushed Sam from our second-story window when he complained.

She did things like that to that man all the time, like busting him in the face with her fist or kicking him. I would hear her say later how she took after her own mother, who didn't take nothing from no man.

Sam would shout back at her occasionally, but mostly he tried to reason with her. I know he wanted to respond in kind sometimes. Yet he never chanced damaging his treasure, upsetting her enough to leave. She was worth the physical abuse he suffered.

Again and again we moved, dotting the small Hispanic area on the outskirts, then back into the more densely populated areas. Our last move was into the Bottom, a section of twenties housing just below a stretch of the Trinity River, which also ran through Oak Cliff. Down there, Sam left us. My mother had poured hot cooking grease on him. I guess that shook him up. Wherever we moved, though, whether five or ten miles away, Junior kept his job. He would walk there through biting storms or freezing cold for the few dollars.

While our escape from the projects had eased some problems, it had sprung others, like all this moving. The more we moved, the more we realized we could never get the family engine cranked. Education slipped farther away. My real mother, who was inside that woman, the person with the infallible wisdom, appeared less. I was stealing. We still had no guidance, had never had guidance. And each time we relocated physically, we became more entangled mentally. We had been away from the projects less than a mere two years. But all too soon, the confusion of our lives was being agitated greatly.

8

MARRIAGE

In 1985, an Italian restaurant in glittering downtown Dallas hired me as a busboy. Being fifteen and still underage, I had to lie on the application; and the circumstances left few alternatives. Nothing would keep me from having my first job on the payroll. I went down to interview for the job after a friend had told me to rush over there because the restaurant was hiring. They were offering first-come, first-served jobs. So I had jogged straight to the restaurant, knowing the place would be stampeded once word spread among the anxious black teenagers. I had entered the quiet restaurant shortly after lunch hour. A white man gave the interview. The only question I remember him asking was my age, without even looking at me. I was hired on the spot with two other boys. It didn't take much to qualify for these jobs.

I was excited and naive about my new job. I walked out the front office believing that with my busboy position, I would provide all the clothes and things I needed and had been missing, especially food. My starting salary was $3.35 an hour, five hours a day ($100 per week), but I didn't care. That was like a million dollars to me. I had been given rocks to eat all my life, so this sand was like steak.

With this job, I also got to see the Dallas I wasn't familiar with. Downtown had the big-city stores, expensive restaurants, and a wide variety of boutiques and shops. Each time I went there, I was overwhelmed by the sheer splendor of the skyscrapers and busy people walking up and down the crowded streets: the whites in their starch-stiff gray clothes, most of the blacks dressed casually or in work uniforms. I would hang at a corner or let my bus pass several times, so I could watch the crowds and gaze at the buildings.

I also located the uniquely designed central library, which had several spacious floors with thousands of books. Before and after work, I would go there, grab several books, and glue myself to a chair in some corner. Later I applied for a library card and began taking my books home with me. Over the past two years, my reading had slackened, but at this library I regained the former pace.

On the other end of downtown was the two-story restaurant. Pipes were exposed on the ceiling, and old artifacts decorated the lobby area: statues, telephone booths, coin games. Spacious bars were on both floors.

"More bread at that table. This couple needs more water," the mostly white, gay waiters would shout to us black and Hispanic busboys, dressed in our white T-shirts with the restaurant's logo printed on the front. The busboys were responsible for keeping fresh bread and water on the tables, seeing that ice bins and water pitchers were filled at each workstation, and quickly cleaning the messy tables after customers left.

I stayed busy at work and became friends only with the black dishwasher. I was so gratified to be working until I only had time for my job; besides, if a busboy worked very hard, within two years he could move up to five dollars an hour, I was told by the hiring manager.

I was so happy to be receiving money, I sometimes would look at my check stub over and over. My family had been without steady money for so long that I believed I could make a living working at the restaurant the rest of my life, that the job was the jackpot, and not a stepping-stone or a means to an end. I was so desperate for money that the weekly mediocre checks seduced me. The stealing stopped. And the job became my life for several months.

This was in 1986. My mother and I were living with an elder named Wayne*, whom my mother and I had been with for several months. She had wasted no time after Sam packed his bags and went home to west Dallas. She had told us to gather our belongings and had a man take us to Oak Cliff, to the house of a man in his late sixties. When I first walked through the door, Wayne had given me that all-too-familiar glare, the kind that said "If it weren't for your mother, boy, you wouldn't step a foot inside my house."

Wayne was a gray man, the stubborn kind who would argue with you all night about anything he thought was true. Each Sunday morning he performed his deacon service at some church, and each evening he drank wine with his old buddies at the corner house. Wayne, in the beginning, was like the men in the past, in that he had no interest in me but was tolerant because of my mother.

And I was aware of the sacrifices my mother made, staying and sleeping with men like him so that her children would have a place to stay. I knew she still had her womanly desires, to be loved and held by a man she really loved. But most of the ones who accepted us were unattractive, drunkards, elders, freeloaders, or dope fiends. If not for her children, she could have gotten into better situations. Many of the high shakers would have loved to have her. Wherever she went, though, no matter how lucrative the offer, she would never accept unless her children were included. This motherly responsibility, thank God, was still a part of her.

We moved into a damp wooden house on Denley Street, near the Veterans Hospital. Here, our living environment went down another level, for the house was in terrible condition. There was little insulation and no heat, so cold seeped easily through the walls. When we first moved in, the toilet didn't work, forcing us to use a bucket instead. The house smelled constantly of dead rats, rotten food, and body waste from the bucket in the bathroom. Cooking was done on a small hot plate, and since we had no refrigerator, food was kept in an ice chest. But my meticulous mother attacked the dirt and smell in that house until it was tolerable.

I slept in the small back room on a mattress filthier than the one I used in the projects. Since my room was closest to the bathroom, the grotesque smell stayed back there, even after the waste bucket had been emptied. My body fevers, which had stopped for a while, came back. The sickening smell nauseated my soul.

My mother and Wayne slept in the front room, where a small electric heater gave them warmth. She and I rarely talked. Our relationship was just one of toleration. That person wasn't my real mother anyway. She stayed gone with her dope fiend friends for days, in the neighborhoods where heroin was more concentrated. She drained Wayne of his money. But, of course, he didn't care, as long as his fine young woman was with him.

Shortly after we moved in with old man Wayne, Junior left. He dropped out of school and enrolled in the Job Corps. While waiting on his eighteenth birthday, the qualifying age to join the Job Corps, he stayed impatient, having heard all the wonders of the government's advertisements about Job Corps, the real chance. On the day after he turned eighteen, he was on a Greyhound bus to San Marcos, Texas, hastily wanting to find this opportunity. My sister, whom I seldom saw, still lived with my aunt Cheryl. So I was the only one of my mother's children still with her.

I became a slave to the restaurant. Since I was required to punch in at a designated time, I would begin without punching my time sheet, giving the business free labor, hoping to impress them. Once the regular time began, I would work feverishly without taking breaks, bringing water to the mostly white customers, keeping bread on the ten or fifteen varied tables (which could hold from two to ten people). If a busboy could clean the tables rapidly and help the waiters satisfy the customers, the waiters would tip him. To stay ahead, I tried to have the tables cleaned before the customers left. Eventually I was deemed an exceptional busboy. The waiters would try to get me into their stations, which meant happier customers and, therefore, more tips.

The gay waiters there despised us blacks, the way I had seen whites do in the past. They would turn their noses up at us busboys, even if they were gay, and flirt with other races. I foolishly had believed gay men did not have enough people to choose from to be that selective. I remember my conversation with one waiter in particular, the first person to tell me that I was a minority. I was baffled to learn that we did not represent at least half the American population. He told me that his preference for white males had nothing to do with race, but more with his view that few black men were middle class, his social class, and he wanted to date someone with the same background. Several weeks later, a new busboy, a Hispanic who was not middle class, let us all know one day in the kitchen that this same white waiter had propositioned him. His problems with blacks, whatever they were, proved stronger than his sexual desires.

I became so skilled at being a busboy that on Sundays the managers would let me bus the entire ground floor of the restaurant—covering an area that usually required three or four busboys—all alone. I think the management also had plans of making me a porter because they made me receive maintenance training from the Hispanic porter. But before I got that far, they found out my age.

After the manager fired me, I was disappointed for a few days. Being able to buy food, give my mother money, and catch the bus downtown were the things I would miss the most. After I lost my job, and since I had quit school, I hung around the house more. Now all I did was read, clean up around the house and in the front yard, or watch my mother.

She was becoming very secretive about her activities. On the days when we were at home together, she would get dressed in some of her better clothes and walk down the street. I watched her do this for several weeks but thought nothing of it. I figured some man was showing her a good time. But while she was somewhere out there, something had moved her once again to give her religion another try.

She had joined another church. As I have mentioned, the church had revolving doors, and the constant promises of peace and happiness preached by the ministers always drew people like her back for another dispirited tangle with the religion. But whenever she was inspired to try to redeem herself, whether a member of a church or not, she became caring and sweet.

I believed these infrequent times of closeness between her and me always made up for the weeks and months of neglect. During them, she would talk to me about my childhood, about as a baby how curious and mischievous I was.

"You would keep somebody up all night with your questions, if they let you. You wanted to know everything," she said. On Denley Street, I still had questions.

"Momma, why can't you get off drugs?" No longer attempting to hide the problem from me, figuring I was mature enough, she would explain how heroin affected her.

"It's a physical sickness unlike other dope," she would say. "That's the reason it's hard to kick, because of the sickness it gives you." She said how important it was that the person stay around positive people if they ever did kick. "If you go back into the same neighborhood, into the same situation with the same people, you get right back on drugs. I have left heroin alone plenty of times," she told me. "I know I'm wrong for what I've put my children through. I try and try, baby, but I just can't do it all by myself. I hope my children can one day forgive me."

Over the next few weeks, perhaps inspired by this growing relationship with her son, maybe stirred enough to try to bring respect to herself, to heal her gaping wound, she continued going to church and staying home more, pacing the floor at night, sweaty and sick. Something I thought I would never live to see was happening. One day at a time, week by week, she was leaving the dope alone. I was encouraging her and buying her womanly things like stockings and perfumes with the little money I had. But I think she knew her death was imminent if she did not change soon; knew she would either succeed in freeing herself or die.

Perhaps compelled by this desperation, she took her efforts farther than I had imagined she would. She came home from church one day and shook up the shack house on Denley. "Wayne," she said, "I can no longer continue in this adulterous relationship with you. I'll be moving out soon. I'm getting married."

9

FORGED

The city bus maneuvered its way through the rush-hour traffic of downtown as I sat on the backseat, holding the trash bag filled with my clothes. Normally passengers were required to transfer to another bus to reach their destination. But this one was going straight through town and into south Dallas, where my mother and her new husband lived. So I remained on the 44 Oakland route, on my way to my new home.

I had thought I would remain with Wayne and begin my adult life from there. After his heart-wrenching separation from my mother, he had deemed me a good kid, told me I could stay with him as long as I wanted. But my mother moved in with her aunt-in-law until she was married and called two weeks later to tell me I could come and live with her; evidently, even while she was at the church, she and her new husband had been planning. With the passion of Romeo and Juliet, my mother and the deacon of the church had eloped, I was told. They had attended church more than usual, sitting there eyeing each other.

The church, if it could be called a church, had only four members: a preacher up and coming, who had just begun to build his flock, his wife, and the deacon, the preacher's friend. My mother's choices were rather narrow. The minister's wife was my mother's aunt-in-law, the sister of her father, information I didn't learn about until after the marriage. She had been picking my mother up sometimes from the Denley house; the deacon had come, too.

Given the circumstances, I can see why they waited only two months after they met to get married. He was fifty, had three children, and was divorced from a nearly two-decade marriage. And he was another man compelled by the beauty of a fine woman, as so many men are, and insanely jealous. Having worked for over thirty years on the same job with a respectable salary, he could offer her everything she needed. He wrapped her up before some other older man did.

At this stage of her life, my mother was at the climax of her battle with the heroin demon. Wayne, the man we had just lived with, didn't have the resources to support my mother and her children. Furthermore, he didn't attend church as much as was necessary for her. Alvin* was the best choice.

As I sat thinking, the loud, crowded, dirty bus continued through town, then onto the overpass over Interstate 30, and finally to the Oakland bridge. I was nervous.

What made my mother and her husband choose a house in south Dallas, I don't know. Its notorious reputation as the toughest section of the city had even reached west Dallas—it was rumored that the men who had come for Shortleg Lee were from here. Surely it wasn't the safest neighborhood they could have chosen. As the bus began descending, the dangerous beauty of south Dallas was laid out.

Oakland stretched straight ahead to where its end could not

be seen. It was busy, like a Hollywood boulevard. A liquor store and a club were on the right, where about thirty men were conversing. Across the short street, another ten or fifteen persons had gathered around a barrel in which a fire kindled. They lounged on thrown-away couches, among deserted clothes, bottles, hypodermic needles, and car tires. Farther down Oakland, the bus continued, passed Good Luck's Hamburgers, the Martin Luther King Community Center, dance clubs, and endless rows of slum apartments, where small families and single mothers lived. Kids stayed out late at night around here—running, playing, looking. Liquor stores and pawnshops were as plentiful as grass and trees. Some of the pawnshops had "Open Twenty-four Hours" signs on them, as if a law-abiding person would wake up at three A.M. and say, "Oh, I guess I'll go pawn my TV."

I hopped off the bus at Oakland and Twyman, then walked swiftly down Twyman until it changed to Lenway. Finally, on a brown sign beneath the mailbox, I spotted the right address. In surprise, I double-checked the numbers. It looked more like an unoccupied church—it had glass, double doors, and monoliths upholding the front porch. But a small door with an air-conditioner unit was at the adjacent corner of the rectangle. I knocked on the door.

I was beckoned in by my excited sister, whom I had not seen for nearly two years.

"Hey, Jerrold!" she screamed out. "Come in, boy. . . . Look at how skinny you are. I thought you would have grown by now. I see you still got that thick hair, with your black self."

Sherrie had dropped out of school while living with my aunt Cheryl but had gotten her GED, or equivalency diploma. Afterward she had worked several jobs, paying our aunty Cheryl a monthly fee.

Since my mother and her husband were not there, Sherrie showed me around the pleasantly decorated duplex. She, twenty, had matured into a young woman. We exchanged hugs, and she showed me where to place my trash bag. I had not expected to see her. She said our mother had told her all about Alvin, and she had known about the wedding plans from the beginning.

Sherrie happily showed me the house, starting with the living room, which was in the front. It was decorated with two small couches, a lounge chair, and plenty of rugs, lamps, and pictures. In the middle of the room, a small door led to the next room, which had two beds on either side of the wall. Another small door led to my mother's bedroom. The kitchen, bathroom, and back porch were beyond another door. It all felt very homey.

My mother soon returned with her new husband. "Hey, baby," she said as she grabbed and hugged me. I immediately noticed that she had gained weight and her worry had eased. She smiled broadly. I could tell she was no longer using drugs. She introduced her new husband, who also gave me a pleasant smile from his round head and fleshy face. He was short, his eyes small and his head bald. He stood back and looked at me, appearing humble, with his hands clasped together in front of him. Together, and with the impression of the house, they looked like two Quakers.

In the beginning of my days on Lenway, I was left alone, encouraged to look around the neighborhood and help myself to the plethora of food in the two refrigerators. Two refrigerators! My mother warned me, though, that I was expected to enroll in the local high school, James Madson. I was sixteen and had been missing many days of school, attending about one-quarter of each school year.

Over the next few weeks, I explored south Dallas on the several buses assigned to this section of town. The 44 Oakland route continued past Lincoln High School, down Bexar Street to the rough Bonton projects. I rode the 14 Lagow and 12 Second routes, which both passed by the state fair of Texas, the east Dallas projects, the Dixon Circle hood and active Hatcher and Second streets. I saw Lincoln High School, from where the young students would walk down Bexar, Hatcher, and Oakland, curiously watching their people.

South Dallas was a paradox to me, far from my expectations. It was where I would be forced past normal restraints, with my efforts for survival, where I would mature into a man.

Among other things, south Dallas had a diverse mixture of people: neighborhoods full of elders who wanted nothing more than meager survival; young men who were a breed tougher, more violent, less tolerant; young ladies with children who desired only a basic, poverty-level home. South Dallas also had the others, the ones who were less satisfied, who were persistent in their attempts for the white American way of life, the security. They desired to live comparative with technology at that time. They felt swindled out of happiness, forced into lifetimes of sickening poverty. Their missions were those of redemption, extrication, using whatever tactics they saw fit—robbery, drug dealing, schemes. Unlike the ones who performed these acts for survival only, these people did so for other reasons. I would come to know many of them personally.

I enrolled into school and into the job program, so I could leave school early and look for work. Although my mother had some excess money now, she still wouldn't buy me school supplies. She felt I was old enough now to get things like that for myself—I kept my simple clothes washed and pressed.

The routine at the house was fairly straightforward. Alvin would work all day, then spend the evening in his room with my mother or at the church. My sister worked all day doing housekeeping for a hotel and spent her leisure time visiting friends, her new boyfriend, Marcus Greer, and going to church also. And I mostly went to school and, afterward, would engage in teenage interests.

On my first ventures into the neighborhood I met Eric, who attended Lincoln High School, where he played on the basketball team. He lived several streets away in a crowded apartment with his many brothers and sisters. He was about my age, sixteen, and still learning the streets like me.

Eric piqued my interest in basketball. We would go to the Martin Luther King Center, or to Wheatley Park, to shoot hoops. Often, people from the neighborhood would have big jam festivals down at the park, loud stereo systems: the lusty young girls and the hardened young men, who would be relaxing and cooling in their reefer and forty-ounce high. Everyone played the emerging rap music. Tempers stayed short; tension stayed high.

I was with Eric when I drank my first beer, more out of curiosity than anything else; I hated the taste. The drinking age was still eighteen, and we both looked eighteen, so he and I would buy forty-ounces in the morning before school and after we had played a hard afternoon of basketball. This was all too common among most of us young naive boys, who were venturing more, becoming more streetwise.

Around then, too, my interest in girls was growing. I especially admired the dark girl with shoulder-length hair who walked past my house each evening after school. I would make sure I was in the front yard, raking leaves or trimming the bush near the window when school let out. She was really developed for her age, narrow waistline and shapely thighs and hips. She seemed shy, would swiftly walk down my street while being escorted by a young man.

One day, my courage strong, I stopped her. I told her I had been watching her and wondering if she lived nearby. She said yeah, and that she had been watching me, too. She said she, as she passed with her brother, would ask him if I was watching her. We exchanged phone numbers, agreeing to call one another.

We began to talk on the phone or in person after school, sometimes for several hours. Her name was Lisa*; and she and I had a lot in common. We both were quiet and not interested in more than one relationship. Neither of us had had any serious social experience. She was still a virgin.

She lived with her aunt, one street over, who had a lot of

relatives living there, because her mother had some psychological problems; and her dad didn't come around. Lisa was required to do a lot of house chores, since her aunt was letting her and her brother stay there. This was common among black families, that a relative would be treated as a subordinate or constantly intimidated if he or she had nowhere else to live. The relative either took the unfair treatment or moved.

Lisa was so sweet, flashing her beautiful, sincere smile all the time, humbly putting up with her problems. I visited her at her house all the time. Her family—cousins, uncles, and all—liked me, thought that she had made a good pick. So Lisa and I began a relationship.

I met another person then, too, who, unknown to me, would become a close friend. We met after my reputation as a pretty fair rapper had spread through the neighborhood. I had begun doing things like that in my spare time, writing rap lyrics and poetry. I recited my lyrics one day at the park before a crowd of about fifty people. And the people really liked it.

Vernon*, eighteen, also wrote prolific rap lyrics. He was a very serious person and also dangerous—he had shot people. He was so surprised that a new guy in town was impeding upon his unblemished rap fame that he came to my house and asked to hear my lyrics. Standing about my five feet ten, he listened, evaluated my lyrics, then recited some of his own. He was good. Later he told me he was forming a rap group, and once more details developed, he would get back with me. I liked him, so I told him to keep in touch. Who knew, maybe we could attract some serious attention.

But one night Vernon came to my house nearly in tears. Men in Grand Prairie had shot his young female cousin to death, and he was trying to gather his friends to get revenge. I thought about going with him, was flattered he considered me his friend. But we were not that close, not yet, anyway.

News of death poured in after I heard about Vernon's cousin. First we received word about the tragedy of Ms. Ruthy Mae, the old junk lady from the projects. Her daughter, Sweet Baby*, had been bringing tricks over. After Sweet Baby ran off with one's money, he bashed in Ms. Ruthy Mae's head with a hammer while her granddaughter witnessed the whole horrible thing. The killer took and tied the little girl to a tree. After several hours, some guys noticed and untied her. She ran home screaming for her grandmother. Relatives later came and took her away.

A week later we got the news of my uncle James's death. He and his wife had separated but were living in the same neighborhood with each other. I was told that she had been dating a white man who also lived nearby. Uncle James, who was short and stocky, got into a scuffle with this man. When he slipped, the white man pounced on Uncle James and stabbed him once in the heart as he lay on the ground. I felt for my three little cousins, who now would be split up among the family.

As Vernon and I grew closer, I visited him at his house more often. I soon found out that as a youth he had lived in the projects—the sections in the projects were so big that people could live there for years and never know each other. This gave Vernon and me a deep familiarity and respect for each other, even though he had spent most of his teenage developing years in south Dallas. Around his duplex house, I was surprised by how much his family shouted at one another, Vernon especially. They constantly, angrily debated everything. Even Vernon's little sister, Yolanda*, a straight-A student and a pretty little girl about nine years old, would scream her lungs out.

Vernon's family was among the elite among the tough blacks of south Dallas. His father was feared at the prominent prison he was held in. Both his two uncles—one small, one average-size, both in their early thirties—had been to prison several times, yet not for some hothead crime, the kind young, ignorant people committed. They were the kind of men who could put a gun into a man's mouth and blow his brains out without the slightest remorse; men who had wrestled police officers about to murder one of them; men who were way above average intelligence, who understood this system and society better than most people. They were the type who would lay down their lives at the drop of a hat for what they believed in and who would remain loyal to a true friend until death. They reminded me of my older friend in the projects, the cool brother, in that they had a hidden knowledge and lore. Vernon had learned much from their settled, unflaunted wisdom. I would learn from them also.

In another way, they reminded me of other people I knew. For Vernon's uncles were both on dope real bad. One was an expert thief. He would go downtown and come home with sacks of clothes. His other uncle had been in prison over half his life. He also stole and sold, or traded, the merchandise for dope. For all their wisdom and common sense, they didn't have the power to implement one thing. They had been silenced and snuffed out so thoroughly.

I was spending all my time away from home, either with Lisa or with Vernon. Eric had become more occupied than I with his love of basketball. Things were looking up. I had buckled down at school, was gradually improving. My mother was doing fine. And my sister was working at a day care center.

Lisa had begun to come over to my house. My mother realized I wasn't very sexually active, so she would try to keep an eye on Lisa and me. But we managed to be alone several times when my mother was at church. Because of her responsibilities at home, though, Lisa and I spent more time at her house.

In December 1986, the winter weather was still around, and everybody stayed bundled up. Lisa invited me to a Christmas party her family intended to throw. Word was around the neighborhood that she was my girl, with my always being on her street and all. And Lisa and I were growing closer, sharing deep secrets.

For example, she had a very masculine uncle who really approved of me. He often wanted to take me aside for small conversations, which never aroused my suspicion. "Jerrold," Lisa said, "I want you to be careful around him. I'm not going to tell you why. Just trust me." I immediately figured he was gay, and Lisa admitted this. But he's not exactly that, she said. He likes both men and women and, sometimes, children, she told me.

Although I was too ashamed to let Lisa see, finding out he possibly had violated a child evoked the sad incident from my past. After Lisa's revelation, I became uncomfortable when I visited her. So we would sit on her porch more, instead of inside the house. She was content with this, being the understanding person she was, but she made me promise to come inside during the Christmas party. She was all excited about some of her distant female cousins, whom she wanted to introduce to me during the party.

The way a lot of blacks celebrated Christmas in the poorest, toughest sections was not how one might expect. Christmas carols were not sung, mistletoe was not hung. Instead, everybody would glow from strong liquor. Strong black tunes would be played, Johnnie Taylor, Bobby Bland, Latimore, and so on. In a smoke-filled dim room, the old heads (elders) would get on the floor, grinding each other with those old dance steps; the younger ones, in their early twenties, would be just as laid back and settled. A couple whispering to one another in a corner. A fat lady working her hips and big behind, dancing with somebody's drunk daddy. Liquor bottles everywhere.

On the night of the party, Lisa came to my house, looking all pretty in her makeup and tight jeans. I was looking forward to drinking with the older folks and maybe doing a rap for them. I had not been to many house parties, so I had that youthful excitement. I was so anxious to get rolling that I didn't pay much attention to what was going on at my house. I had been staying away too much to notice the settled changes; yet when I left, my mother was sitting in the living room reading her Bible. Like an omen, her twisted worried look had returned. That was odd, I thought. There was no need to worry; everything was fine for her. I made a point to ask her about that later.

At the party, Lisa's family was cooling all the way when she and I arrived. She introduced me to her female cousins and their older boyfriends. Then she introduced me to her male cousins, who had brought their dates along also. After a short conversation with them, Lisa grabbed my hand and led me through the haze to meet one of her special cousins, who was sitting in a corner with his girl. At first I thought something was very familiar about his girl, her posture, her slim figure. But I could hardly see her in the dark, until she turned to greet us.

It wasn't too difficult. Some residue of her still remained. She was still kind and gentle, still greeted me with her soft, compassionate voice. But the rest of her was in terrible shape. She was filthy. Her hair was wild, her clothes dirty. Now on heroin, she had drug marks on her arms. And her eyes had changed, now had that same reflection of betrayal, the way she looked on the day I blackened her eye. Why had this happened to her, to the first girl I had ever kissed, who had shared my first small flame?

Gloria recognized me but was too ashamed to keep looking, although she did murmur a wry hello and offer a spiritless smile. I spoke to her, wanted to pull her to the side and find out what had happened. But I didn't because of her jealous boyfriend. I left the party early that night.

Few things in life have shocked me more than seeing Gloria destroyed. During my stay on Lenway Street, I never shook the ill feeling, the dread, she gave me. She had been so sweet and wanted so badly to make it out, but, once again, she lacked self-reliance. So she had been forged and pounded into a dope addict by the circumstances of her life. Gloria had followed in the footsteps of her mother. A normal, natural thing to do.

10

MIND WILDERNESS

When she began to leave the house at odd times, I knew my mother was back on drugs, that the snare of her past was reeling her in, by the same gradual pace in which it had freed her. Alvin was ignorant about this, and neither my sister nor I told him, thinking it was just a temporary setback. Why was she doing this? Alvin was treating her well, and everything had been going okay. As well as I knew my mother, the cause avoided me, until I came from outside one day and Big Mary was sitting in our living room.

"Hey, there's my handsome nephew," she slithered.

I stopped dead in my tracks and looked at her intensely for several moments. But there was nothing I could do. I knew my mother would defend her with a dope fiend's loyalty. So Big Mary was the reason. She had moved to south Dallas and sniffed my mother out. She had hunted her down and caught her during her weak stages.

And once everything was in the open, Big Mary kept coming around; so my mother kept slipping away. She was desperate now, praying all night, fasting for weeks at a time. But nothing worked for her. She had been on heroin so long that the slightest disruption threw her life in disarray. And Big Mary was a strange woman.

I just stopped seeing Lisa. I couldn't let her know what I was going through. I wanted and needed her kind support. But I wouldn't return her phone calls and letters. She had enough problems. After several weeks she stopped inquiring, and later she moved away. Within two years Lisa married a young man, joined the minimum-wage work force, and had a son.

Soon my sister moved away. Then the skeletons came out of the closet and chased my mother around the house. She sold everything except the kitchen sink. Alvin just couldn't understand. Saddened, he would ask me what was going wrong, why my mother was in need for so much money. But I couldn't tell him, couldn't do that to her.

He put things together and got my mother to confess her shortcomings. Now, I had been sympathetic of Alvin up to this point—after all, my mother had hid her past from him—but what he did next hurt her more than anything. He abandoned her, just packed his bags and moved away while she and I were gone. My mother must have known that this was coming because she didn't miss a step, getting back on dope after his departure. If he had given her some real support, I believe she could have pulled through. But he left and took all the resources with him.

Sherrie had found a new job working at a day care center and was getting more serious with her new boyfriend. She knew, as I did, what my mother was up to, and she was also very disappointed. After Alvin left, my mother charged my sister rent and tried to squeeze all the money she could from her. As loyal as my sister was to our mother, she eventually became fed up and moved in with her good friend Pam.

I left school again and returned to the industrial, factory streets of cheap labor. I had, after a week or so, luckily stumbled on a maintenance position for a carpet cleaning company, minimum wage, of course. It was two hours away on the city bus.

I worked about twelve hours a day, then another four hours catching the bus, in the beginning. I would get up about four A.M. to get there around six-thirty. The company only had about ten employees. I had many responsibilities. I worked in the warehouse, cleaning and sorting the equipment, stacking big barrels of chemicals. In the offices, I cleaned, vacuumed, dusted, and took out trash. I also cleaned the four bathrooms, their all-around handyman.

Yet there was no way to pay for all the bills—lights, water, rent, phone, food—in a house while making minimum wage. So I begged a foreman to let me try cleaning carpets. After I received several days' training, I would work in the evenings after I had completed my day shift. We cleaned carpets at night, when most businesses were closed. I would go with the white men and let them assign me the undesired chores, scrubbing on my hands and knees for hours. I stayed quiet, never complaining. Sometimes I worked until after midnight and even later. The buses stopped running after midnight, so usually one of the employees would give me a ride as far as downtown, from where I would drag myself home. Later, the sympathetic owner gave me a key to the building and let me spend the night whenever I worked late. I would curl up near one of the desks and try to keep warm—they didn't run the heat after hours.

My mother was doing all she could to support me besides leaving heroin alone. She would cook my supper and wash my clothes. Even if she was out on a heroin adventure, there would be several pots on the stove when I got home from work. I had taken up the position as man of the house. And this was something she had done for every provider in the past.

I kept the job for a while but eventually was laid off again. It seemed to happen every time. Before I left, I begged the owner, who didn't have the nerve to tell me in person but sent his assistant, not to lay me off. I told him I understood he was having hard times, that I would work for free until things got better. Although impressed, he couldn't do that. At home, I couldn't tell my mother I had lost my job, I was so ashamed.

She made everything easy when she came to me one day as I was pretending to leave for work. "Jerrold, I already know, don't worry about it, baby. You've been trying real hard. Momma got some ideas to help us get on our feet," she said.

Her idea was to rent her bedroom out, mostly to male tenants, who would hit on her. And even though I kept telling her getting involved with them was the wrong thing to do, she dated a few of them. I came close to fighting one of them, a heroin addict named Mark who stole car stereos. He told her some stupid story about his wife just passing away, and my mother wound up being compassionate toward him. In the end, he paid no rent.

My mom tried to work, too. She was hired at a temporary maid service, cleaning up after conventions. But the work was temporary and not enough. We were near being homeless again. With all the money and morale vanishing, she took her only alternative. She called a thrift store. And she called Big Mary. I don't know who got there faster, this white man who knew he was about to make a killing off some poor desperate black, or Big Mary, who had the same ambition. My mother and Big Mary sold everything in the house for about two hundred dollars. She was going out with a big bang, a big heroin party.

Motivated by the new proceeds, Big Mary agreed to let my mother live with her—she knew having my mother around would generate more dope for her. But where was I going to stay? I certainly couldn't go over there. Unknown to me, my mother already had worked out a deal. "Big Mary said you can come, too," she said.

I had no intention of doing that. I told her not to worry about me; I would find somewhere to stay. Her worry lines popped in her forehead. "Baby, Momma thought you were gonna come with us," she said. "I understand that you don't want to be around her, but what are you gonna do? This may be our only choice for now."

I would rather have been homeless than move in with Big Mary. I was afraid of what I could become being in the same house with her. I decided I was going to just stay right there in that empty house until I found another job.

My mother seemed saddened, seemed to have not figured I would reject the offer. But after I assured her I could make it on my own, she packed her clothes, gave me the address and twenty dollars. "In case you change your mind," she said. We then exchanged our last good-byes.

The first week, I started off okay. The landlord didn't know we had moved. I would get up each morning and go through the want ads. I would try to visit all the different spots on the city bus. Up until then, I had been able to find work on the first or second try. But I soon learned just how difficult it could be without basic resources. For example, the labor jobs for which I qualified usually were dispersed all across the wide city. In a day, I could expect to visit maybe two, which required impeccably correlating the bus schedule with the days and times the companies allowed interviews. Then the long bus ride there, which sometimes only came within a mile of the place and sometimes ran every two or three hours.

My fate usually was decided before I even interviewed. I could hardly help but be late for the appointment. Some required tests. I would be so hungry sometimes that I couldn't read a sentence. And most of the jobs also required that the person have a car and phone. Each time I was rejected, my morale crumbled.

Back in the house, in the frigid, dull nights, I rationed my food to a snack or two a day. I slept curled up among the trashy mess—paper, boxes, clothes—left after the hasty move. Then the electricity service was cut off. Then I came home one evening and the doors were locked. So I slept in the back shed. But on the second night back there, I realized I was only delaying the inevitable: Big Mary and Dixon Circle.

The next morning I began the walk to Dixon Circle down busy Second Street. Before long, B-boy*, a person I had met around the neighborhood, drove up and offered a ride. Man, I was happy to get out of that two-mile walk. On the way, B-boy acted strange and paranoid, kept looking around the car. He suddenly shifted his attention to me and asked did I want a bump.

"What's a bump, man?" I inquired quietly, hoping it was food.

As though he had been hoping I would give him a reason, he pulled onto a dark, vacant street and retrieved something from under the seat. He placed the glass object, which had a thin rod, a stem, to his mouth. While holding a lighter to the pipe, he drew long and hard on the stem. The pipe glowed, hissed, and turned dark red like old blood. Full of satisfaction, he relaxed, leaned back, and asked again: "Do you want a bump?"

I declined. I had seen weed smoked in pipes before. "Why do you call your weed a bump?" I asked.

"This ain't no weed; it's rocks," he said.

"What?" I asked.

"You've never heard of rocks, Jerrold? Yeah, fool, rock cocaine. It's here now, man, everywhere."

11

STAY ALIVE

On Dixon Circle, in the midst of the seated young men, Fat Travis slammed the domino onto the small table. "Three ladies went and got raped," he said. Fifteen points.

I shouted, "That's the way to hit their asses," and reached for my can of malt liquor, on the dirt near the leg of the table. Working on my sixth can of beer, I felt good. The opposing team contemplated their next move, giving one another signals about what each player had in his hand. Fat Travis and I were ahead by fifty points. We weren't worrying about winning. We were more concerned with blowing them away.

As usual, a crowd had gathered around us domino players, some older men, several girls, but mostly younger boys. Popey, a man in his early twenties, was the partner of a skinny Dixon Circle teenager, who was a usual. This was the normal ritual for us. After a day of getting up early in the morning and catching the bus downtown, if we had gathered enough bus fare, where we roamed separately all day, looking for work, we sat out and played Bones.

To try to find work, we would walk around depressed south Dallas, inquiring at the foreign-owned grocery stores, the small mechanic shops, the pawnshops, or the schools for any type of work—janitor, sweeper, standing in the heat or cold holding a sign all day, pumping gas, washing cars. We didn't care if the pay was ten dollars a day or five, just so long as it was enough to buy food, energy, strength, bus fare, enough to try for something better tomorrow.

And after an exhausting day of this, or early in the morning if we had chosen not to battle the impossible task that day, we would sit down with our forty-ounce beers, sixteen-ounce beers, always hard malt liquor, the kind that really gave us an alcoholic buzz. Sometimes we sat out there and played dominoes from early morning until late evening, the winning team staying up, the losing team waiting until their time came again. Why not? The houses were smoking hot early in the morning, enough to melt a man. I can't see how anyone stayed in them, how the smaller kids sweated in their shorts, skinny limbs tangled together on some mattress. They were suffering.

We huddled together out there, healing ourselves in a way known only to us and in a way that did not hide our disgrace. For we were well aware of what was happening to us, seemed to sense the silent effects, the molding of living in Prince Hall Apartments on Dixon Circle. Since there was no economic relief or opportunity, no morale, no way out except by selling dope, becoming a criminal, waiting on that long-shot miracle, some of us chose just to exist and not sell dope, to just keep giving what we could to improvement, but not to push ourselves to the brink of death and insanity anymore. Our minds and bodies already had paid dear enough prices.

This wasn't America. This was famined Ethiopia, desolate Somalia, or any of the other sub–third world countries. Dixon Circle, south Dallas, west Dallas, nothing but concentration camps where economic, food, transportation, health, and housing sanctions kept us, for the most part, confined and subdued.

Yet some of the boys were saying to hell with this suffering. They were grabbing the one and only commodity in existence, rock cocaine. They refused to sit and starve, to watch themselves, their families and mothers, go to waste. With the arrival of rock cocaine, however, which came into the neighborhoods so easily and swiftly, they said to hell with these impossible odds. We'll sell dope until the shame of our naked hunger is covered, until the wicked are punished with sulfur and brimstone. We'll dance, make love, sweat on each other, and eat crack until we are resting in the earth.

"Bolts and screws," Fat Travis screamed out. Twenty points. That gave us more than enough for the victory. Our fourth game. We were on a roll, for most everybody was a skilled domino player. Rarely did one team win four consecutive games.

The young boys were watching us older teenagers in the busy Prince Hall Apartments; we were their role models. They saw how we quit school, played dominoes, stole car radios and lawn mowers, and sold dope. They were learning from us.

I told Travis I'd had enough for today. He complained, since I was his regular partner, but he let someone else substitute. Fat Travis was Big Mary's oldest son. We had become good friends over the three months I had been here. Meanwhile our mothers had become con partners: they used their wit and duplicity to trick people out of their money.

Big Mary had a daughter, Tracy, who reminded me of my sister, in that she cleaned, cooked, and took care of her smaller brother and sister. Tracy was still trying to go to school at Lincoln—from where I think she did finally graduate. Tracy always got on Big Mary's case about not taking care of the house and her two younger children. Big Mary would humbly agree and say she would improve. I was surprised by this. But that was the understanding between a depraved mother and her righteous daughter.

I was adjusting to the perils of Dixon Circle. No one had a choice; you either learned to survive or perished. I had become more skilled at fighting, as everyone ignorantly took their anger out on each other; a lot of the hotheads, troublemakers, stayed ready to fight. And with the dope had come the random shootings and murders; the strawberries, girls on rock cocaine; and the more desperate, more cunning men on rocks.

The dope dealers began appearing everywhere in south Dallas and Dixon Circle, one, two, and three to a corner, a hot spot, a rock house. But these weren't the big shakers and rollers, nor were they the dope fiends who were paid dope instead of money. Instead they were somewhere in the middle, the boys from the poverty families, the few boys who made enough money to say, "Damn, man, we made it out of poverty, at least temporarily." But a few of them were slipping through the cracks and making thousands of dollars: the fancy cars, the gold, the houses.

In the beginning the money was so fast, the business so lucrative, that there was plenty for anyone who wanted to sell, wanted to risk imprisonment and death. Some youngsters made three and four hundred dollars by just being lookouts, others five hundred dollars for selling the rocks. You could choose to sell alone or work with an organization. The ones who worked alone stayed small, maybe selling a few dozen rocks a day.

Along with the emergence of rock cocaine came the hard-core rap music—not the mellow rappers. They rapped often about selling dope, the glory of its success, how they had robbed, murdered, kicked, AK 47 sprayed down, Uzi'ed down, beat down, pimped girls, fucked up niggers, and slapped bitches. A lot of us, especially the upcoming dope dealers and the younger generation, were absorbing these messages, having them reinforced over and over again through the music we people loved so dearly, the rhythms and beats we enjoyed so much. Our minds were so raw. We did and acted just like the music programmed us to do.

The people who got on rock cocaine, the strawberries and rock stars, the Apple Jacks, became chaotic. We—the ones not selling and the ones selling—had to watch out constantly for these fiends, who were killing themselves over the dope. Heroin was a lunch snack compared to rocks. Once a person got on this dope— it usually took just one try—you could say good-bye to him. All day long the fiends would buy the ten- and twenty-dollar rocks, which only gave them quick squirts of relief, maybe lasting fifteen minutes. Then it was time for another ten- or twenty-dollar rock. These fiends were so desperate that they would boldly take or steal whatever they needed to get the rocks, putting their lives in constant danger.

But the young ladies and girls suffered the most. For they had one thing that could always bring them the next hit: their bodies. They would roam up and down the streets near rock houses and flag down men with rocks or men who would give them the money for one. They would roam for days at a time without sleep or food, like zombies fulfilling an ancient biblical prophecy or curse. They were easy to recognize. Their bodies usually had dried up to skin and bones. The dope dealers, and a lot of other men—preachers, husbands, boys—were taking advantage of them. "Give a strawberry a rock and she will give you what you want," was one saying. The men had their pleasure, several men for a rock or maybe a bump. I even saw a young kid give a woman a rock to perform a sexual act with another woman behind an apartment in broad daylight, while a crowd of onlookers watched and laughed. It was a sad and perilous time for young black women in the extremely poor areas. It was an aphrodisiac night-mare.

What is more sad is that everyone was instinctively aware of what was taking place, of the destruction; of how a lot of us were going to jail, to the grave, or being irreparably damaged in some way. It was like being securely tied to the earth, wide-eyed and alert and watching a herd of ants slowly taking your body away, bit by bit. A few of us would talk about how bad things were getting or discuss who had begun selling dope.

"Shit, ain't no other way, man; everybody else is making some money. So let me get mine."

"You know how wrong that is, man. Look at what's happening to everybody. I'm not going to do it."

I, myself, thought long and hard about selling dope. I wanted to get involved, make enough money to go to school and to move away from Prince Hall. I was losing my respect for society and everyone. The white police officers constantly harassed and beat the crap out of us; the businesses wouldn't hire us; we couldn't get higher education. So my reasons for living, for caring, for resisting, were leaving, one at a time.

Lo and behold, though, as she had done many times before, my mother rescued me, came from out of her secrecy to preserve my life. She saw how I had stopped looking for work, how I was no longer concerned with anything, how my drinking had increased, and how I was spending more time with the worst crowd.

For example, she and Big Mary had swindled some man out of his money. He came to Big Mary's house. Big Mary came to the back room, to where Fat Travis and I were, and told me he was waiting in the front to hurt my mother. I grabbed the big pipe from under the bed and charged into the living room, while Big Mary tried to keep my friend, Fat Travis, from joining. The man must have heard the commotion, because he scrambled out the door and disappeared. I'm certain that if I had reached him, I would have beat him to death, or he would have shot me, and one of us would have gone to prison, the other to the grave.

Each morning my mother began walking to a neighbor's and making calls, trying to find a place for me to go. Before long she came up with something. Regardless, I wanted to stay there with her, but she told me to go ahead and leave and that she would be okay. She even had a driver whom she had paid waiting to take me.

After leaving Prince Hall, I moved in with an old man and his wife, two die-hard Christian friends whom my mother had known for years, the same man who had come in the church van and taken us to Sister Hill's house that summer. He lived several streets from Dixon, so I still would go to see my mother and friends.

I stayed there only a week or two before we became intolerant of each other. But my mother made more calls, and I soon was living with my aunt Cheryl in Oak Cliff, the aunt who had kept my sister. Cheryl's husband had a good city job. They lived in a three-bedroom house in a black version of a suburb. She had four children, two teenage girls and two younger boys.

I already had completely stopped drinking when I moved in with my mother's friends and had regained my motivation. With Aunt Cheryl over the summer of 1987, I mowed yards in the neighborhood and used the money to look for work. I found a job at a convenience store in Pleasant Grove, just east of Oak Cliff.

Now, as I have stated, it was strange living with relatives, especially if they had the slightest impression that they were better and socially more advanced than you. They began to treat me like an outcast, a disgrace, a black sheep. I was required to do more chores than anyone else. I was constantly fussed at and threatened with eviction. Although I didn't have bus fare to get back and forth to work, they refused to lend me any, even though I had found a job. After I began receiving paychecks, I was required to give at least 25 percent of my earnings, sometimes more. I sometimes ate, sometimes didn't. They took glee in not saving or cooking enough food for the black sheep.

But these things didn't bother me. I walked the five miles to work and then back late at night. One of my aunts, Cheryl's sister, lived directly behind the store. One day, when she was on her way home, I asked her for a ride. With an expression that said she enjoyed treating me, this project black, like shit, she said no, and that she didn't have to explain her reasons. I walked again that day.

On another day, her husband, Tony, came into the store. He saw how hard I was working and felt it was his duty to give me a word of advice. "Jerrold, you might as well stop working so hard. It doesn't matter what you do. You'll only get as far as the white man lets you." I argued against what he said, didn't believe it. But his words stayed with me.

One day after walking home from work, one of my aunt's daughters swore up and down that I had been smoking weed. It was a straight-out lie, by design, an excuse to get rid of me. It hurt me, and I could not understand it. But I was so sick of the place that it didn't matter.

I talked with my aunt Felisa, the sincere, down-to-earth one. She lived along the way I had been walking. She said I could come and live with her for a while. So I moved into the shabby Sherwood Garden Apartments, which was about a mile from the store and a much easier walk.

This aunt had five much younger children. She was downtrodden poor but still was kind enough to let me stay there. As recompense, I let her get groceries from the store and put them on my charge list. I also gave her generous amounts of my earnings.

At the house, my sister came by one day to see me. She was pregnant and was getting married to her boyfriend, Marcus Greer, who had grown up in Oak Cliff. I wished her well and told her I hoped everything worked out. I figured she could handle a kid; she would be twenty-one when her little girl was born in 1988. She told me to stay in touch. She later moved into a drug-infested apartment complex in Pleasant Grove, another part of Oak Cliff.

Meanwhile, my brother had returned from his six months of Job Corps training. He moved in with a distant cousin in the Prince Hall Apartments. He was so disappointed when he returned, finding out that most companies thought his Job Corps mechanics training was a joke and didn't really consider Job Corps graduates. He had been fooled by the government's propaganda. It was all a waste. Now he was over in Prince Hall, suffering.

At the store, I again was exerting myself beyond normal. The first day, I worked a graveyard shift. I was instructed to clean the parking lot. I scrubbed on my hands and knees until I bled, picked up every piece of trash in the surrounding brush, along the street, and at the back of the building. When the manager came out to inspect, she said she had never seen the lot that clean in all her years with the company:

I went on and worked hard at the convenience store, pulling double shifts, sixteen hours, becoming so fast on the cash register that the manager would often stop and inspect my receipts. She doubted that I could program the gas module and insert the prices while giving the customers direct eye contact. When the store was not busy, I would go through it in a blaze, mopping, stocking, dusting, and cleaning.

In the first month I won the customer service award and an outstanding review by the customers. The district office called the store and said to the manager, "He even has customers calling this office with praise," something that had never happened.

The district manager was very pleased. He took me into the office with the white female manager and told her to start teaching me how to do paperwork. "You're a very sharp young man, Jerrold, I want to one day send you to management school." Things changed after that meeting.

At work, the manager started acting strangely. She told me my work was not good and that customers had been complaining. I couldn't imagine who would have complained—I had become a skilled ass kisser. She wouldn't divulge her sources but one day accused me of stealing and said if I got one more complaint, I would be fired.

I was so devastated. My hopes had gotten so high, I thought I could become a manager and go back to school. I knew she was intimidated and was harassing me because of this. And she accused me of stealing! Up until then I had not dared touch anything in the store or let anyone else—and I would quickly defend the store against the young men who did steal, compromising my own safety. I knew she was going to fire me. So before she could hammer down her death blow, I quit and then took me some money.

It was fall 1987. I was seventeen, but most people thought I was in my early or mid-twenties. With nowhere else to go, I headed back to south Dallas.

My mother had moved out of Dixon Circle and into a duplex with a man who lived on Latimer Street. It was several streets from Lenway on the other side of Oakland. Once I contacted her, she suggested I come to live with her again. I was glad to get back to the old neighborhood.

In south Dallas, she was living in a paint-peeling duplex with an older man. The elder, whom I nicknamed Big J., had been living at the house for more than sixteen years. He was a retired plumber and owned land in an agricultural part of Texas. He had successfully raised several children, children who never came around. Anyway, he stayed in a good mood. He was in fair shape to be in his eighties, walking each morning down to Oakland, to drink with his friends.

In south Dallas, I got back with all my friends, the camaraderie on the corners and at the Ice House. Each evening in large groups, we got together, the ages ranging from fifteen to eighty, and talked about life: what was going on, who had become pregnant, gotten shot, gotten murdered, went to prison. We discussed our philosophies about life and women, listened to the old heads, the elders, who knew a lot about everything. In these coversations, which were loud and lasted late into the night, everyone would share his deepest conviction. Everyone knew he was a marked man. Everyone was trying to beat the odds and stay alive.

12

CLOSED LORE

The spring of 1988 had arrived, and already the duplex was hot. In the front room, the coffee table sat next to the dirty chair with flat armrests. Pieces of old furniture and pictures decorated the walls. The curtains were thick and blanketed the windows. It was dark, so dark I had to feel for the door that led to the only bedroom, where Big J. had clothes bagged in trash bags and stacked everywhere.

From in the living room of the duplex, among rows of other duplexes, I watched the girl in the private school uniform get off the city bus that ran down quiet Latimer Street, which crossed with Metropolitan and Atlanta. She was small and short, with smooth skin and thin legs. She had on her private-school skirt and dark shades today. She walked around the corner and out of sight. One of these days I'm going to get to know her, I pledged.

I took a back trail behind the house, down to Vernon's. I was spending more time at his house, as though I were a family member. The house had two duplexes, one in the front (his grandmother and uncles) and one in the back (his mother's). His brother Jonathan*, who usually roomed with him, was living with a girl in Grand Prairie. His mother and stepdad liked having me around, thought I was a good influence on their radical, dangerous son. His mother and grandmother always told me in private that they wished Vernon would follow my example instead of trying to rob and take everything.

His mother worked full-time, and his stepdad worked odd jobs. I often slept in the extra bed over there, more than on my couch at the duplex. Vernon, every now and then, would read. He read the Bible and other books on religion, his aunt's college books on math, medicine, and other subjects—she had gone to a community college for a couple of semesters. His uncles had read voraciously also and had a collection of books in their room in the front duplex, books we used.

Vernon and I were growing in curiosity, intellect, and discernment. But this was not caused by any teacher, any school, or any role model, because none of them existed; and we both had quit school. Although from time to time we would catch glimpses of the sixties experience from the old heads, their personal challenges and failures, the wisdom they had gathered through years of confrontation, most of our passion, our desire to know, our sense that something was terribly wrong with all of us, came from within. A dormant force, an internal conflict, a sleeping thing.

We often expressed our views in the rap and poetry we still wrote in the back room. Everybody in the neighborhood admired it. Vernon often wrote about the twisted times he saw, and he had two favorite pieces:

> *Don't let this world mislead you, refuse to go astray.*
> *Sad is the brother who for the love of an illusion would*
>   *throw his life away.*
> *So many brothers and sisters die for nothing every day.*

Wise is the man who dares in his heart to find a better way.
The suffering is so enormous, the pain is so intense.
We die like rats in a cage at each other's throats, in a
    world that makes no sense.
Frustrated and angry we get as we go round and round.
Lost in an insanity, where can truth be found.

He went on and wrote:

Rise, unite, and awake.
Strengthen the mind of the blind, so that they may come to see
. . . Life is too short to live and die in vain.
Don't live your life in vain, hating and spreading pain.
Love each other as thyself and to thyself be true.
Do unto others as you would have them do unto you.
Each one, teach one.
Tell the children man is mind and allow them to find the
    true design.
Rise, unite, and awake.

From Vernon's back room, we also planned robberies. Vernon influenced me, and others, to try robbery to get money and resources. He felt that my inspirations were a waste of time. He was a devoted atheist, and we had countless arguments on the existence of God. And after many of these discussions, he finally agreed that God must exist and agreed to work on his relationship with God.

But that same rebellious character made him believe we should just take what we wanted. So we became stick-up kids, something Vernon had done before. I had hustled up several guns. I bought a .38 revolver from a dope fiend for twenty dollars and purchased a used twelve-gauge at a nearby pawnshop for under one hundred dollars. I had turned eighteen, the legal age to purchase shotguns.

Vernon, other young men, and I would rob some place, get us a big booty, and live off it for several months. We only robbed foreign- or white-owned stores, which we felt were sucking the community dry anyway. We robbed department stores, fast food restaurants, service stations, and the hordes of small Asian-owned grocery stores. Sometimes Vernon robbed dope dealers, whom we classified with the whites and foreigners. We usually grossed a few hundred, sometimes over a thousand dollars. Afterward we would split the money. We also had vowed never to sell dope. We saw what it had done to our families and what it was doing to the neighborhood.

The few robberies weren't a big deal, were really rather funny. I usually was the lookout or driver. We always took our time, evaluated the risks, location, getaway routes, alternative plans, and levels of danger. I had gotten a penal code to determine which types of robberies were more serious than others. And I consulted Vernon's uncles, who were experts. We never got greedy, never got caught, and never harmed anyone.

With our booty, we would give our family members and friends money and gifts, even though we knew some of them would waste it on dope. Vernon was so compassionate. He would do things like rob some store and give all the money to someone who couldn't pay his or her rent, not leaving one dollar for himself. We would give our friends money to get them some beer. We would buy ourselves a new outfit, a rap tape, some Thunderbird wine, or beer, weed, and food. Then we would relax a little, meditate, think, and, sometimes, get enough motivation to look for work again. We were like Robin Hood, in that we took what we needed and gave to the poor and took from those who were robbing us anyway.

Neither Vernon nor I went out, dancing, movies, and all, but mostly stayed in his room, reading and talking. Sometimes we rented a room from a nearby notorious motel, where we would invite our friends to relax for a while or invite our lady friends.

The neighborhoods in the south Dallas communities were close this way. All the young men and women for several blocks would be close with and concerned for each other: Willie, Michael Ray, Tabaras and Lee Roy, Shon and Tasha, Elvis, "Dog Daddy" Wayne, "Big Daddy" Kevin, and many others. It was not uncommon to find us sitting on a corner or at someone's house, drinking, tripping, laughing, and eating or discussing the news or events in the neighborhood. We were like a big family.

Vernon smoked weed. I, too, began to smoke weed but stopped after about six months—and he stopped a little later. We would quit drinking altogether for a month or so, then maybe start back drinking a few cans a week. We hardly ever got drunk, just on a few occasions when we misjudged the alcohol. He and I both could cook, he much better than I, and we ate heartily at his house.

We also were the protectors of our families. We and our friends, who lived on the nearby streets, looked out for one another. Everybody recognized this unspoken code, that everybody from the "hood" helped each other fight—including girls. At any time of day I could roll up in the neighborhood and round up six or seven guys, who would lay down their lives for me. And many times I would go somewhere and be willing to lay down my life for my friends. If a stranger came to the neighborhood to start trouble, which many did, he could easily find himself being kicked and stomped by a dozen people or having his car riddled with bullets.

The main reason this closeness existed between us was that none of us looked for trouble and everyone did everything possible to avoid it, at least in the Ice House neighborhood. So you knew, when you were called, that fighting was the last alternative.

Vernon was a natural warrior. I was a creative fighter also. We would practice late into the night on ways to, say, disarm someone with a gun or how to react to gunfire or a knife attack or in a fight in which we were outnumbered. We evaluated, and criticized each other's techniques until we were very skilled. But we never became bullies. Instead we used these skills to guard against the youth who were being pumped up by the hard-core rappers and crack glory. They were getting bolder, ignorant, and more dangerous each day. They were killing a lot of people we knew.

Besides these activities, some things touched me to the depths of my heart, like singing on the corners. Two or three evenings a week, we would gather on the corner at the Ice House: Vernon's uncle, Gregory Taylor*, one of the old heads named Eugene, Sammy Ray, and his brother Regis, who both were from the struggling group Destiny, right out of south Dallas.

We would buy us several forty-ounces to loosen our cords, form a semicircle, and get the rhythm going. We sung old Stylistics, Marvin Gaye, Blue Magic, Teddy Pendergrass, Sam Cooke, New Birth, and the Isley Brothers' music. When we really got hyped, we would just make up songs right there, and everybody would fall into place, Sammy or the old head on lead, Regis and Greg doing background, or vice versa. I had what the old head called a fifth, able to hit notes off the scale. We would harmonize a chorus, each voice falling into place; and when they had blended and were holding a tune, I would throw in that fifth, and the harmony would melt everybody.

People going into and coming from the store would stop and listen; all the young boys would gather around to request their special love song. The owner would stick his head outside sometimes, giving his nod of approval. We would go on and on, singing and laughing, sometimes late into the next morning.

I convinced Vernon, after months of discussion, that the only way we could become successful would be to go into business for ourselves, create our own job security, work hard, seek a higher education part-time, keep up our reading and private study. My mother agreed with this, encouraged us, and said to let her know how she could help. Vernon's uncles, his aunt, his grandmother, the old heads, all agreed. Everything began to fall together.

Vernon got in touch with his half brother, Shelvin*, who had a friend, Jamie*. Both were in their early twenties. Shelvin, Jamie, Vernon, and I were at the same crossroads in our lives.

We all had worked like dogs on jobs taking us nowhere and had grown up in west Dallas. They, having earned a contract in the local school district, had started a small disk jockey service. They were trying to raise money to begin a small record production company. All of us were seeking the same thing, a way to success without selling dope.

We were hardened, so we all shared similar qualities, such as motivation, endurance, discipline. But we had our distinct qualities, some a lot stronger than others, and our faults, too. We drew strength from each other.

Shelvin, for example, had a shrewd sense of fundamental business. Short and muscular, he was dedicated and compromising. His mother had been murdered in west Dallas, and his daddy, his and Vernon's daddy, was an uncaring man. Shelvin could be discouraged quickly and depended heavily on us for support. Jamie—who had done several semesters of college before running out of money—was a whiz at math and management, all natural. He was from the minimum-wage group and sometimes was stubborn, egocentric, and not a team player.

Vernon was intelligent, wise beyond his years, and fiercely loyal. Yet he stayed frustrated, impatient, far too arrogant and violent. I had a knack for understanding complexity, strong organizational skills, and an accurate memory. But I could get too emotional, distracted, and sacrificial. And I preferred isolation. We all read a lot, but I probably read more than they.

In the midst of the madness, we were very serious about forming a business. This was not uncommon. I have said in the past how most people I knew, all the ones I talked with, had once had the same high ambitions, high goals. Some of them were foolish enough to try and almost lost their sanity in the process. Others looked at the fools who did try, or sensed enough about what was in store, and simply refused to try. Better to have some peace of mind than be a bitter, warped, rejected, depressed person the rest of your life.

Ironically, a week or so after we had begun meeting, Vernon

almost knocked my door down at the little lime duplex. I reached for my pistol until I heard him call my name. I let him in. He jumped around, blurting his words out. He was coming from a meeting that Jamie had encouraged him to attend—Jamie was learning more about Islam and thinking about becoming a Muslim.

"Man, I just came from this meeting," Vernon said. "You should have been there, man. We heard some powerful black people speak. Some of them were Muslims. They had on these long robes. They were dressed so death [impressively]. They had people there from all kinds of organizations, man. I got the number from this one man, Fahim Minkah. We're going to go to his meeting this Friday."

Vernon was so excited because he had just seen for the first time in his life people whom he thought really cared, could really do something, who hadn't gotten out and become Uncle Toms.

On a Friday, we piled into Jamie's car and drove to an apartment in Oak Cliff. We were going to get advice on our ideas. We were invited inside by a nice man, who had arranged several chairs in his living room. Several people already sat around. Outgoing Jamie and Shelvin were mingling real well, while Vernon and I stayed quietly seated. Soon, Fahim Minkah arrived.

Fahim was keen looking, tall and gray-bearded, like a wizard. He smiled broadly, and his eyes gleamed with knowledge. He quickly took control of everything, stood before us, and spoke.

"My name is Fahim Minkah, formerly Fred Bell. I want to welcome you all here today."

He talked a very long time. He mentioned an organization he was about to start and how important it was for blacks to become economically self-reliant. I got the impression he was there to recruit people. I sat there quietly, amazed to know he even existed. Clearly he was skilled with words and accustomed to speaking. And sincerity sprang from him like sunshine. Toward the end of the meeting, Fahim angrily stated that we were going to do something about all the crack houses. Afterward he inquired with us for more information on just how bad things were. He was somewhat detached from the deeper levels of poverty.

Jamie managed to mention our desires to start a small business. Fahim, and the man who lived in the apartment, said to keep them aware of our progress so that they could help us. They offered no advice at the time. But they both agreed that self-employment was better than working for white people.

Vernon and the rest of us would all try, as many had done, to defy our poor origins, without sacrificing the community, hold on before fate sucked us under. We agreed to meet every Tuesday to try to start a business, to get out, get some resources, bring some life into this dead, sleeping neighborhood. But we all were so fatalistic and overwhelmed by the sheer magnitude of this undertaking. We would try, though, until it brought us close to despair.

Back at the duplex, I finally had gotten around to getting that girl's phone number. Her name was Tammie. We had been talking often on the phone and before she went home after school. We also spent time together in my living room, when I wasn't with Vernon or the fellows or writing poetry and essays late into the night while watching for crack-head burglars.

Tammie, sixteen, was an only child and had been raised, mostly, by her grandmother. Her mundane, materialistic mother had taken over and passed on her values when Tammie was a teenager. Tammie's personality was sweet yet clever, her mind ready, her heart inexperienced.

She was a nice girl and really admired me, even though she was from a more fortunate background. Her mom hated me and tried to stop her from seeing me. But Tammie was a rebellious sixteen-year-old who had been watching her fifteen-year-old cousin, who lived with Tammie's grandmother one street over, go to all the parties with all the boys she wanted. Tammie wanted her teenage life and would do whatever it took to get it.

After Tammie's mother found out she was seeing me, she told Tammie her all-too-familiar "You can get out." That day Tammie gathered her clothes and went to her grandmother's house, as she had done many times before, where she called to let me know she was okay. But, after this time, she would never again move back with her mother.

On many nights, Tammie and I lay in that dark duplex, sweating on each other, sweat mixed with a fervor untouched by any wrong. Unlike many young couples in the neighborhood, we were serious. We were spending a lot of time together. Times were pleasant. I was excited about the possibility of success, and this helped us with the relationship. Even though we were opposites, Tammie and I had grown close. She would not let anyone keep her from seeing me. "But, Grandmother, I love him," she had said one evening. Her family began to accept this.

I stopped being with my friends so much once she entered my life. We could often be found at the Hardemans Barbecue on Oakland, where they still remember us today. We would sit in there and eat, and play the jukebox, and do the same thing at the Ponderosa on Pennsylvania Avenue. When I had extra money, we sometimes spent nights at motels. Tammie didn't drink, but she wasn't bothered by the beer I like to have sometimes. To support our relationship, Jamie and Shelvin would pick us up in the mornings and take us to breakfast sometimes.

She didn't care much for them, my friends, and would often want me to choose between them and her, wanted me to be with her all the time. But I always managed to divide my time up in a way that made everybody happy.

I would meet Tammie downtown, to ride the bus to south Dallas with her. I had never been much for going out, so when she wanted to go to a ball game, party, or formal dinner, I would stay home. In a way, I never thought I fit that form of teenage life-style. I had way more experience on the streets than Tammie, and I preferred, instead, the small, close gatherings with my friends, with whom I felt comfortable and safe.

Tammie seemed to be the perfect addition to my life. Her concern for me seemed genuine, and at the start she was very supportive of the ideas I had. Then one day, only three months after we met, the troubles began. I was about to learn a valuable lesson about the power of a woman and the priceless bond between a man and his child. While we played on the couch one afternoon, her shirt flew up. I saw the little nudge in her stomach. She was pregnant.

13

FAILURES

After Tammie and I confirmed the pregnancy at Dr. Mason's Clinic on Martin Luther King Street, from the depths of my mind sprang the deeper passion.

Deeper than my love of privacy, deeper than my love of my own life. It was a calling of manhood, of responsibility, of too much knowledge of children abandoned by their parents, deceived by their parents, abused by their parents, good children, manipulated, hurt, molested, and molded by an organized society, deserted in their most urgent times, left to chance a ruthless environment.

From the moment of confirmation, heredity took over. This was me, a man, a black man, all black men, to either accept or deny, nourish or suppress, love or scorn, the child. It was nature, human, godly, all these things, to know that I was appointed the director of this life, as my mother and father, as their mother and father, even as the first mother and father had been.

Whether it meant sacrificing high ambitions, slaving as a blue-collar laborer, miserable and depressed, or running away completely, choosing not to be responsible, giving up the ghost, choosing not to comfort my own hurt in the godforsaken life, I had to choose.

As I would, many teenage black fathers chose to be responsible. Many did not. The latter were everywhere in the neighborhood, denying their Pampers- and milk-lacking babies, denying the desperate, burdened girls. These were the young, hopeless fathers who abandoned their children, ignored their needs. Rather than face another failure, knowing their ragged lives could only take so much, they refused to try.

The thoughts were in my mind, and I chose, just as surely as there is night and day, to be a true father. It was still spring 1988. Tammie was only four weeks pregnant. I had some time to sort out a plan, however much that trouble would assail me.

Tammie and I both agreed that an abortion was out of the question. We wanted to just be responsible and do the best we could. But I could tell she was very, very scared. She had come from a spoiled background, with a wooden spoon—a good poverty spoon—in her mouth. She was afraid yet was trying to be brave.

She decided to keep the pregnancy hidden from her family for the time being, and so did I. Hopefully, everything would work out with the things I was trying to do with my friends, which I discussed with her in detail. And maybe we could move together. She believed in me.

At Vernon's small duplex, we had combed through every idea from a car detail shop, a small record store, a small grocery store, and a record production company. We chose a record shop, wrote an outline, and even caught the bus around west and south Dallas to look at some possible sites.

Needless to say, nothing ever got off the ground. The first

major obstacle was money. We couldn't borrow any—not with our zip codes and lack of collateral. Our parents didn't have money. We didn't know any investors. Jamie did draw up a couple of proposals, which, I believe, he submitted to some small loan, government, and business entities. They were laughingly rejected or caught up in some bureaucratic process. The only way we were going to get any money was to take it.

But we had completely stopped the stick-up kid business and were reluctant to start again. However, Vernon, with his by-whatever-means-necessary attitude, was pushing for one last robbery. He was fed up, irritated, and restless—word had gotten to Jamie's concerned mom, my mom, and others that Vernon had us selling dope for him, after we had tried to encourage him to choose another way. Vernon did one last job, a department store, and netted about $1,500.

We split the money, each person vowing to keep his lot per the plan, and continued our research. We soon learned that $1,500 could hardly buy us buckets and mops, much less pay the lease, registering cost, and the rest and still leave us some money with which to feed ourselves and give bounty to our family members. Stuck, we consulted Fahim, who had no money and suggested we consult some of the same entities we already had contacted. And, he added, he was a very busy man.

We did service a party at Lincoln but got into a big fight with some dope dealers. A young dealer was staring hard at Vernon, the kind of stare men use to dignify their manhood. Vernon wouldn't stand for that under any circumstances. He let the cuss words roll. The dope dealer pulled a gun and chased Vernon through the crowded gym, then through the back door. I followed behind the two of them. Just as the dealer was about to point the gun at Vernon, I put him in a choke hold. He lost consciousness and dropped the gun.

Meanwhile, Vernon was sprinting to his house to get our guns. At the scene, having run outside, I had placed myself among the dealer's friends, who reacted. When I rose up, one of them hit me hard on the face. By this time, Jamie, who had been spinning records, had come to my aid, hitting the guy several times with a pipe. Jamie and I fought our way back into the gym. Afterward, the police came. Everything was spoiled.

Around the house, Vernon's mom was getting tired of his attitude and had threatened to put him out. His uncles were constantly fighting, causing trouble, and keeping the police around, who would harass everybody. Later, Shelvin's sister, whom Shelvin had been living with, put him out because he wasn't working. He moved in with Vernon, and Jamie was such a loyal friend that he left his own house to come and suffer with Shelvin. We used the money to eat and live, the four of us. They spent the nights, sometimes sleeping in Vernon's room, sometimes sleeping on the floor at my duplex. We would give my mother ten or fifteen bucks to keep her happy. Big J. was happy if she was happy.

Vernon's mother did eventually move away from the commotion her brothers kept up, even though she wanted to stay close to her mother, with whom her two brothers and sister still lived. Vernon chose to move around to his grandmother's rather than move away with his mother. This forced Jamie to go home and Shelvin to go back to his sister, who accepted him. Later, Shelvin foolishly tried to rob a store by himself. The details remained vague because he got caught, and we couldn't talk to him in jail.

We were all depressed about our failure. However, we pledged never to give up hope and to try again when things were better. But for now, we all would go our separate ways.

Over the next eight months, Tammie and the baby became the center of my attention. I found an evening, part-time job cleaning office buildings downtown. I would meet her each evening at the bus stop on Latimer, where we would talk about our plans before she went home.

She would skip school on the days of her doctor appointments, I was proud and determined, and already nature was forming a bond between the baby and me. Always on the corner, we would stand for an hour or so, comforting one another, me doing most of the comforting. Her bulge had gotten bigger, and her face had become puffy. I even would feel her warm stomach, standing out there.

My brother had begun coming around to visit. He was looking for somewhere else to stay besides Dixon. With no alternative, he had joined the navy. All along, I had been hearing about the dozens of boys I knew from the projects, Oak Cliff, Dixon Circle, and south Dallas, who joined the service. These black boys weren't joining freely and willfully. They saw right through the transparent lies the armed forces told about success and opportunity for blacks. I believe the armed forces knew that the poverty-stricken black boys joined for the hot meals and warm beds. Most of them were coming back to start where they had left off, nowhere.

With my mother, I should have known things wouldn't hold together too long. No matter where we moved or how much things had settled down, it never lasted long. My mom had begun stealing money from Big J., who was on a fixed income. I would get into shouting matches with her for abusing this good man. She would threaten to make him put me out, but Big J. wouldn't. So she began staying away, two and three days at a time, because I wouldn't let her exploit him. Big J., who knew she was on drugs, was very appreciative. He told me I would always have a place to stay as long as he was around. To get even, my mother, from wherever she was, sent people to steal his checks.

Consequently, the lights, phone, water, and gas were turned off. So I used my cash stash, about five hundred dollars, to get everything reconnected for him and me. He was so grateful, he was almost in tears when he learned what I had done for him. But things got slow at the part-time job, and I was laid off.

I cooked and cleaned for Big J. until we ran out of food.

Fahim, late into the night, would bring us dinner from his own table, after I had swallowed enough pride to call him. Fahim said I should never hesitate to call him in times like that.

Partly through my curiosity, partly hoping he could help me find a decent job, I began spending more time with Fahim. I would go to his house, where I mostly wound up just sitting, listening to him talk on the phone, or running errands for him. He made me pass out pamphlets in front of grocery stores and also to various places where he held meetings. I learned he had dedicated his life to these kinds of things. Among others, he had belonged to a group called the Black Panthers, and he had been wrongly imprisoned. He said the police had framed him for bank robbery, in an effort to silence people like him.

At age forty-nine, Fahim was a very dedicated, experienced man. He didn't have much money and was just a fraction above people like me. Even though he was married and had five young children, he was always on the go, always at some community or city council meeting, giving a speech to a small group or confronting the establishment about something. He was full of charisma, and people seemed to sense he could do wonders if he had the right support.

Fahim was starting a new organization, one whose first objective was to form an antidrug group—under the authority of his parent organization—to confront the drug establishment. It was at one of these related meetings that I learned he was a Muslim (I didn't care; I didn't have much respect for any religions at the time). He took me to this strangely shaped church on Harwood, a mosque, where fellow members worshiped. Although they congregated there with Arabs, the ones we met with were black.

As I sat there quietly observing, Fahim introduced his idea to the black Muslims. They listened while looking stubborn. Although I felt comfortable around them, I immediately disliked them all. They were very discourteous to each other and acted like a bunch of arrogant know-it-alls. Fahim could hardly complete a sentence without some interruption from a man who could not even talk right, much less say something with substance. They all would talk about how manly they were and would try to take the lead with Fahim's ideas. (Later I would hear their spiritual leader on a radio program claiming to have started AAMAN.) Fahim seemed much more intelligent and out of place with them. And but for him, I would have lost all respect for black Muslims.

At length, Fahim suggested to everyone that the serious drug problem needed to be handled first. He said there would be no future to deal with unless it was resolved first. As we listened, he explained his strategy for dealing with the problem, which he called civil harassment of the drug dealers. They chose to launch the first effort from the Martin Luther King Jr. Center.

That day, the group picketed some dope houses. The media, with their reporters and cameras, accompanied the group, gave AAMAN a lot of coverage. And I was interviewed by a TV crew and a reporter, because I was the youngest member of the group, eighteen. After the local churches saw the attention and praise AAMAN received, it seemed they all started clone groups. But the churches had parades with police escorts, while claiming they were confronting the dope dealers.

AAMAN did have some success. But the lure and snare of rocks would prove too strong for their meager attempts. Over time, after about six weeks of patrols, the group disbanded. The men in AAMAN were fearless. Yet they were also suspicious and jealous of Fahim, and of each other, and always trying to get credit if anything positive happened. Some of them had a price, too.

As for Fahim, he seemed to have a drive, almost an obsession, with his organization and not much time for anyone who didn't join. As for the others, they all seemed so confused to me, seemed just as troubled as anyone. While I felt sympathy for them, they still disappointed me, wasting their time bickering while everyone was hurting. I had expected so much more from them. But they were in deeper trouble than me and my friends.

14

BABY JACQUA

It was approaching late summer 1988. Tammie's beautiful brown belly had begun to bulge more from under her checkered, private-school skirt. She and the baby were why I had to keep moving. I vowed that if nothing else, I would make sure that Tammie and the baby had someone to look out for them.

Though no one was sure, people, especially her grandmother, had begun to ask questions—I already had told my mother, who had few words to say but encouraged me to be responsible. Tammie kept telling me it was time for her to move away from there. She wanted to come over and live with me. But I told her the place wasn't fit for her, to give me time to make something happen. Then I tried to talk her into just telling her grandmother, who I knew would be understanding. But Tammie was afraid that her grandmother would reject her.

Since Vernon was the only one of my close friends left in the neighborhood, I tried to spend as much time as I could with him. Yet it was difficult. He was dispirited, had begun smoking weed again and drinking more. He got into a lot of fights. He and I even got into several serious wrestling matches, but we never hurt one another. Finally, one day, he and I stood on his porch after a heated argument, where he told me that I was going to be shot before the end of the year. I didn't pay this prophecy much mind. But he proved to be only half-wrong.

Afterward, just when I was about to look for another job from Latimer Street, my mother called me into her room. She told me men were looking for her and that she needed to get away. I had learned in situations like that, when someone that close tells you this, you don't ask questions; you just act. It's probably something you don't want to hear. I asked her how much money she needed. She said she knew where she could rent another duplex and needed a few hundred dollars to act. We put together a plan.

She knew this perverted white man she could invite over. She would leave the back door unlocked, to allow me to slip inside and rob him after he was undressed. I talked to Vernon, and we agreed to do it together. He was willing to do things like that for me, for my mother, even though our friendship had become uneasy.

Vernon and I had sold our guns, so before she came back we took two knives out of the cabinet. Big J. had several gangster-looking hats hanging on his wall. We put those on, to make the job more exciting. It was a big joke to us, to be able to catch some strange, perverted white man.

We sat in the living room until we heard the man driving our mother to Big J.'s duplex. We darted out the back door. Once we thought she had undressed him, we busted in the room. The man was lying on the bed, fat, naked, pink, and artery looking. He was very scared and very cooperative, having been caught with his pants down, so to speak. Lying beside him, my mother still had her clothes on. We pretended not to know her. Vernon was giggling and making jokes. "Now look at you, got your fat, pink butt in here with no clothes on. . . . Where's your wife? You ought to be ashamed of yourself." He threw in some vulgar comments at my mother, too, to make things look good. And last, he took the man's wedding band. "Let's see what your wife thinks about that, fat boy." Later I felt no remorse.

Before my mother and I moved into the new duplex, Tammie and I sat on her grandmother's front porch. I told her the circumstances, that I would be moving but would keep in contact. She didn't want me to move away, was afraid if I did, I would lose interest in her and find somebody else. But I told her not to worry, that would never happen. "I'll be in walking distance. . . . We care too much about each other to let anyone or anything keep us apart. Don't worry," I told her. But she was crying.

The new duplex was close to Second Street and the Fair Park. We were closer to the dense apartments on Park Row, South, and Warren streets, where danger was more widespread. Just below, a train track stretched along Trunk Street. Our duplex seemed to sit in the middle of a large lot, with only one other house farther down. The other lots, where weeds had covered the land, were vacant.

My mom found her a new, older boyfriend, who moved in with us and would take care of her. He was a charming, easygoing fellow, had false teeth, and worked hard. We were settled within a month.

By then my brother had returned from an unproductive tour with the navy. He had failed the swimming test and had been discharged. He had moved back into the Prince Hall Apartments on Dixon Circle and had completed a free security officer training program sponsored by the government. Although he was working with some dirt-cheap company now, he was all excited about a new job possibility, which included a free apartment at my sister's complex. Anything to get out of Prince Hall.

After my brother said I too could qualify for the three-week security guard training program, I went all over town collecting the necessary paperwork. I enrolled in the same program he had.

Meanwhile, Tammie was approaching her fifth month and didn't know how much longer she could keep the pregnancy hidden. She was ready to leave. Since the matter was urgent, I asked my mother if she could move in. "I've been meaning to ask you if Tammie could come and live with us for a while, until I can find somewhere else for us," I said.

My mother stood over the stove. "Yeah, she can come. But you need to do your part, pay your room and board. I'm getting tired of you grown niggers in my business." It was back to that, back to her being tired of children who had always been a burden.

After I had put my life in danger for her, suddenly I was a grown nigger in her business. After all the money I had given her, she wanted to charge me room and board. I swelled with anger when I responded, "It's your fault. I could have been on my own by now if you'd done your job as a mother, instead of spending every dime we ever got on dope."

She turned angrily away from the stove and faced me. "Well, I tell you what. You can just get out now!"

To let things cool down, I walked out the door and down the street. I wasn't in a position to rebel, so I would just do what I had learned to do while living with relatives. However, I did regret my words because I really felt that it wasn't her fault. She was still on dope, so everything else still came second. She wasn't responsible. Before night fell on the same evening, we talked about the argument.

"Baby, I'm sorry about what I said. Momma didn't mean it." I apologized, too.

On a school day in the fall of 1988, Tammie packed all her clothes and moved in with me at the wooden duplex on Trunk, down by Catfish Charlie's. We were given the bedroom in the middle of the duplex, closer to the kitchen and bathroom. My mother slept in the front room on a couch bed.

I finished the three-week training and quickly found a job doing security work. The pay was five bucks an hour, and the job required that I have a car. I lied and was luckily assigned a post on a bus route. I worked twelve-hour shifts and all the extra hours I could. Since my fevers had returned, and since I often stood out in the cold at work, I came home many evenings very sick, where I would sweat all night next to Tammie. Before long, with the exception of paying my mother's rent and Tammie's doctor bills at the nearby women's clinic, I was able to save some money. I bought a put-put car from Fahim, who had many old cars, and continued to work.

At the duplex, Tammie was miserable from day one. After I left early in the mornings, she would stay in the house all day and deal with my mother. Some evenings, when I wasn't too tired, she and I would talk, go walking, or go to my sister's house in Pleasant Grove. But Tammie was used to going to football games, malls, and movies.

Perhaps the only pleasant times we shared were the boom-bam hours. Each evening around seven, the baby would go happily crazy, paddling her mother's stomach like a toddler in water and balling up in tight knots. She was developing. The more the baby grew, the more Tammie bulged and warmed from the new life. I became attached to both of them. There was nothing I wasn't ready to sacrifice, even if it meant busting rocks for eternity.

Still, Tammie and I fussed constantly. Her emotions seemed so fragile, and I was so ignorant about how much patience was necessary. Even though I cast most of the blame on myself, some things she did drove me up the wall—like refusing to eat properly, since she was "so used to junk food." She wouldn't eat vegetables. She wouldn't drink milk, not until I told her the baby would come out deformed if she didn't change. Then she accused me of caring more for the baby than I did for her.

And in the background, my mother disliked Tammie and what she saw as a snobbish, spoiled attitude. Tammie said my mother had told her she should be trying to help more, maybe get on Medicaid instead of having me pay for everything. My mother also kept us under pressure by saying we needed to hurry up and move. So one day I called Tammie's grandmother and told her Tammie was pregnant. Afterward Tammie herself called and was relieved to find out how concerned her family was. In a few days she moved back home, which was the best place for her.

Our relationship continued to fail as she lived at her house, for there Tammie was back under the guidance of her mother and the influence of her loose cousin. I later learned that her mother even was encouraging her to get an abortion.

As the months went by, we barely saw each other. Maybe once a week, when she had time, she would come by and spend a few hours with me. I would walk to her grandmother's to see her. Tammie did get on Medicaid and began having appointments at the Martin Luther King Clinic. I had been switched to a night shift, from six P.M. until six the next morning, so on the days of her appointments, and since she demanded so, I would get off work and sit up there with her all day. By the time I left, usually late evening, it was time to go back to work. I was a walking zombie.

During the final months of the pregnancy, our relationship was reduced to name calling. I no longer felt her mood swings were just the pregnancy. The last time she visited the house on Trunk, we sat in the kitchen and talked, then argued. Suddenly Tammie blurted out, "I'e been thinking lately. I really am too young to have a baby. I'm gonna get an abortion. My mom said she would pay for it."

As I stood there, all the emotion I had in me, all the fervor I had for that unborn child, came up. As hardened as I was, having faced so many challenges in my life, no starving, no misery, and no sweaty nights, nothing, had struck me harder than her burning words. That baby was my whole reason for living, my only remaining source of encouragement. I had to be something, be somebody, for her. Now she would be taken, and I was powerless to intervene. Before Tammie, there in that bare kitchen, I wept openly.

I wasn't making any sounds, and if not for the tears, my expression probably would have appeared normal. But the tears were flowing like a river as I looked blankly at her. "Please don't cry," she said. "I'll have this baby because you love it so much."

My relationship with Tammie never was the same. She would still threaten me with the abortion when she got angry, even though she was seven months pregnant.

Around then, from out of the darkness, my real mother came again with her infallible wisdom. "Jerrold, whatever you do, leave that girl alone. She has too much to learn about the world. She will never be right for you. . . . You are a good man. You deserve much better. Put all your love into that baby. You hear me? Don't let her keep you from your baby, who'll be here soon."

On March 5, 1989, Tammie's grandmother called. "It's time," she said. I went outdoors. Dallas, Texas, was under an ice storm. Icy snow was falling hard. Everything was snowy white: houses, streets, and cars.

"Leave me alone!" Tammie screamed to the old lady from across the street who was trying to be helpful, as I stood in the screen door. I walked to where she had slumped to the floor and, as gently as I could, took her night clothes off and helped her into her maternity gown. She took several steps toward the door, then confessed she would never make it. I picked her up and carried her to the car, trying not to slip on the ice. Her cousin and aunt jumped inside, and I drove fifteen miles an hour to the hospital.

In the delivery room, her aunt and I took turns by Tammie's side. Labor pains would awaken her, then the painkillers would eventually make her go back to sleep. Her stomach was bulging with life.

Suddenly she announced, "Judy, tell the doctor it's time. Jerrold, go and get ready."

The midwife told her aunt to stay right there and that we were going to deliver the baby right now. I felt that this was the appropriate omen, since all along her family had intervened. After a few gasps for air, and with the midwife snatching the strangling, crisis-causing umbilical cord from around the baby's neck, it was over.

It wasn't long before I stood watching my daughter through a glass window. I couldn't leave, even though I had to go to work, even though fatigue had overtaken me. Vanessa Jacqua Ladd had barely made it and still had a long life ahead of her. I visited Tammie every day the week that minor complications kept her in the hospital. I changed three flat tires in that cold, biting winter storm. In her room, she and I took turns holding Vanessa. One day the black nurse asked Tammie my age. "He's only eighteen! Girl, you better keep him."

Shortly after she was released, Tammie told me the expected. "I'm too young to be a full-time mother. . . . I want my teenage life. . . . to see other guys." Her mom had kept her so sheltered. And after she turned sixteen, I had come along and gotten her pregnant. I understood her need to explore.

But over the next three months, it was hard letting go for both of us. We had become so attached. She would leave, come back, go out, see other guys, feel guilty, and come back again. I was extremely jealous, and this burned me to the core. My mother spoke again amid this tribulation: "Do you want to get Tammie back? Then you're gonna have to pretend like you don't care. Even act like you're seeing someone else. When you go see the baby, even if she has company, act like you're doing fine. She'll straighten up."

I followed my mother's advice, and it worked. I asked Tammie if she still wanted me. After she said no, I told her a final good-bye. During the two weeks that followed, I ate and slept little. She finally called to say she was so unhappy without me and could we try again. We did, but the same problems came back, mainly her wanting me to understand her seeing other men.

She used the baby, too, not allowing me to see her unless she was in a good mood or didn't have plans. I kissed up for a while, until it all became intolerable. So one day I called her from a phone booth. I said, "Tammie, are you sure this is what you want? I haven't been serious about this in the past, but this time I won't be calling you back. I'll only see my daughter, nothing more."

On that day, as I walked home from the phone booth, it began to rain. But I didn't rush. I had no idea how I was going to live without my daughter and without Tammie. I had taken all I could handle. One more major disappointment, and I knew I would give up. But Vanessa had survived. She was here. She would need me. I understood this more than anything else.

15

THE FIRM

Driving down Trunk Street, my old car hesitated. Suddenly a puff of white smoke came from under the hood, followed by jumping flames. I killed the ignition and popped the hood. It was the faulty fuel pump, spewing gas on the hot engine. I tried to put the flames out with an old rag. Unsuccessful, I jogged to the nearest apartment, hoping I could get the fire department out here in time. At the same time my brother was leaving the duplex, so he drove up to see what was wrong.

Minutes later, as the fireman poked through the wreckage of the motor and dash, I realized the car was a total loss. I still owed Fahim one hundred dollars.

"Don't worry about it, man," my brother said, knowing I would lose my job without a car. I sat on the curb and put my hands in my head. "I'll tell the man about you at the apartment complex. Maybe he'll let you work, too."

At length, the man at the apartment complex agreed to give me and my brother four hundred dollars each, every month, and a free apartment for working rotating, twelve-hour shifts, seven days a week. He also supplied our equipment, including two pump shotguns. Even though this was obvious exploitation to me, it came right on time. I didn't want to move to Pleasant Grove, though, because it was far away from my daughter. But I went anyway. It was the best decision I ever made.

On the day we moved in, my brother and I stopped by Fahim's house first, so that I could pay him. As he worked on an automobile, he told me he'd look for another car for me. Before leaving, I asked Fahim a question. "Hey you got any good books to read?" He stopped for a moment, very randomly selected a book from a nearby shelf, then tossed it to me. He stuck his head back under the hood.

I held a weathered paperback in front of my face. On the cover was a picture of a black man wearing glasses. In all my readings I hadn't read anything on a black man before, except for Martin Luther King and his home boys getting beat upside the head and a lady who got really pissed when she had to stand up for a white man, things I remembered from the school textbooks. I recalled, also, a mere paragraph on somebody named W.E.B. Du Bois, who worked for a civil rights group. I looked at the cover again. The man's eyes were on fire. He looked fierce and determined, as if he could call fire from the heavens if so moved. He doesn't look like the type of man who should have worn glasses, I thought. I promised to read the book one day. Before we drove away, Fahim ran to the car and handed me another book. It was a book about the legal rights of a father.

When we first drove up to the new apartments, dealers were standing around. I jumped out of the car with my pump shotgun and made the small congregation of young wanna-be dope dealers leave—they weren't the problem ones. I had decided that no one would sell dope where my sister was trying to live decently, trying to have a family, trying to raise her little girl.

We were given a two-bedroom apartment and were assigned to the black manager, who also received a free apartment. Through the manager, our sister, and other residents, we quickly learned that everyone lived in fear. The manager was glad to see us.

The apartments were some thirty years old, adjacent to each other, and barely occupied. The hundreds of units were filthy and semidemolished. It was a hornet's nest for drug dealers.

From our damp, unfurnished apartment unit, my brother and I walked around with our big pump shotguns, facing down dope dealers. We did what amounted to headache work (young black kids in Dallas called the police "headaches"). My brother was trying to work a part-time job also. We took turns working the graveyard shift. I preferred the graveyard shift; my heart was too broken for me to get any sleep.

Over the months of 1989, when I was nineteen, we stayed there, visiting our sister, working our shifts. I sent my daughter fifty bucks from each check. In spite of everything, my brother and I were still encouraged. And things weren't so bad. The apartment had air, sometimes. They paid the light bill. And we had food.

Still, making $5,000 a year was pure slavery. We knew this. But my brother was so tired that he didn't care, as long as we weren't homeless. I wasn't that content. Whatever it took, I wasn't going to spend my life in that mess. And neither was my daughter.

Over time, I learned from reading Fahim's book that since my child was born out of wedlock, I would have to go to court and establish myself as the father. Once completed, I could get visitation rights, powers, duties, and privileges.

I figured if I wanted to see my daughter, even one day get custody, I had better have a nice place to live and a decent job. I soon began to gradually improve myself, though things went at a snail's pace. I caught the bus to the downtown community college and told them I wanted to go to school. People who had dropped out were required to take the same tests as high school graduates. While I scored low on the math, I got the second highest score on the reading test—I had become an expert at reading. They were very surprised and said I could enroll in the college at the normal level. I was thrilled!

Still, when would I go? I worked all night, and the school was an hour's bus ride to downtown on the pitiful bus system. Only one way: I would have to find another job, a stable job. I needed a car.

I called Fahim, who referred me to a friend of his, Bob Ray Sanders. He was a well-known black TV journalist who knew a lot of charitable groups. It took me a long time to swallow enough pride to call one. But I did, the Junior League of Dallas, and spoke with Maria*. I was brutally honest, willing to do whatever it took. I told her in brief my situation, about my love for my daughter, and asked her if they could loan me a down payment on a car. Understanding, she said the organization couldn't, but she would ask her husband. Days later she called my house and asked for directions. He, from his own pocket, would do it. One of my best friendships was about to begin.

Now, intuitively, I knew not to appear too black around these people. So I put the broken radio on a classical station and practiced sounding white like the black kids at the elementary school. I also knew her husband wouldn't let his wife visit some black man alone. Sure enough, they both pulled up in a late-model car, and I invited them inside. They were neatly dressed and glowing with business and education. Her husband, Alex*, was tall and gaining thick weight in his middle age. He glanced around the house and then quickly looked at me as if he didn't want me to see he had noticed the terrible apartment. They took a seat on the small sofa across from me, tried to look comfortable, and asked me about my ambitions.

"So, Jerrold," his wife began, "I understand that you have a child you love, and that you want to raise her. But how do you plan to do that?"

"Well, I plan to find a better job and go to school part-time.

My main concern is getting in a position where I can take care of my little girl," I said. I was trying not to give them much detail. I felt like if they wanted to help me that was fine, and if they didn't that was fine, too.

While sitting there, though, I got the impression that Alex was very compassionate, even though he tried to look stern and doubt danced around his face. But I think they quickly became convinced that I was deserving, because they only stayed a few minutes. Before they left, they made sure I knew that $600 they gave me was a onetime gift. I made sure they understood that's all I wanted.

On that day, I had not known just how rich and successful Maria's husband was, or that he was wondering how in the hell I was keeping so motivated. We were from opposite worlds. He was in his forties, a golden boy from an aristocratic family, from fine stock. He had gone to school until he was twenty-nine; and he and Maria both were certified lawyers. But that was not his line of occupation, not Alex. Instead he was the big chief, a big corporate boss, on the board, a CEO of a multinational firm with countless employees and contacts. He was handling the millions.

Prior to marriage and Dallas, he had swung his genius around at the New York Stock Exchange, earning at his leisure, wielding the power of his spotless, golden upbringing. After his success, it was time for marriage, Maria, and three children.

Alex called me several days after his first visit. I was surprised to hear from him, as he had established that he had no further interest. That was not the case, though; something was bothering Alex, something he had wondered about all his life and now had the perfect opportunity to determine.

"Jerrold, listen, how are you?" he said, sounding slightly nervous. "Listen, I was wondering after our meeting the other day, about trying to help you get organized, you know, show you how to put together a résumé, and maybe write some letters for you."

I was uninterested in having him poke around in my business but elected to give the man another meeting; hell, he had given me $600. "Sure, no problem," I said.

"Listen, that's great," he said. "How good do you know downtown? Meet me at the executive health club on Griffin Street." He hung the phone up sharply, like a man who knew how to handle a call, almost in the middle of my good-bye.

Alex and I met in this gym's cafeteria. He had just come from working out. He piled a whole lot of weird food—he called it yuppie food—on his plate and we sat down. I knew right away that he was a probing man, full of all that economic, budget analysis and planning work he did. And he loved it.

"Do you know what type of work you intend to do?" he asked.

I told him just work and went on to answer questions about my education, my family background, my religious beliefs—which had been narrowed down to a belief in the Creator, not religion—and my security job and salary. "What!" he said. "That's all you make!"

Alex and I met several more times before things went any further. During these meetings, he talked about religion often, about how the black church was the thing that had kept blacks going, the place of all their resources. I never let him know what I thought of that.

Alex had a hard time believing that one religion was the right one. "Listen, I don't think all those Muslims around the world are going to hell," he said, looking perplexed. Moreover, he was surprised to find out I wasn't deeply religious like most blacks. He and I had that in common.

After this, Alex invited me to his office, a tall building on the periphery of booming downtown Dallas. His private suite was on the twenty-seventh floor in a far corner. In his office, he had a big desk, golf clubs, and a big world globe. He spoke, smiled, and tossed me several examples of résumés, then jogged to an urgent meeting he was late for.

His secretary helped me make out the résumé, and when Alex

came back he got on the phone. "Listen, I have this guy here who wants to work a full work week while going to school part-time. I'll fax you his résumé, and you send it to management." He did this with about five law firms where he knew people. He instructed me to call one week later for an appointment and reviewed, with me, basic etiquette and interviewing techniques: how to talk, smell, dress, and act.

About a week later, I interviewed with five law firms. The interviews were very routine, as if the decisions already had been made. One law firm in particular was expressing a lot of interest. There, I was interviewed by at least five white women.

"What do you think is the most important thing being a case clerk?" one of them asked as they sat around me in the crowded office.

"I think that a case clerk needs to be able to follow instructions, not be afraid to ask if he doesn't understand . . . mind his bosses . . ."

"That's very good, Jerrold," another one said, as if she were talking to a man who had just held up one finger on request— "Yes'm, ma'am, this heh is da one fingu. Gib me ah peanut."

I was hoping and praying that one of these law firms would give me a chance. I knew once they saw how hard I worked, I would never be without a job. It would be all I needed to get in shape, to get my daughter.

In another week, Alex called me. "Hello, big shot! . . . What did you say to them? We got three job offers!"

I told him to hold on, while I got off the phone, turned forty-nine flips, soared to the heavens, and jumped over the moon. "Man, I don't know how to thank you for this," I said emotionally.

"Don't worry about it. Come into my office and we'll go through everything."

I went to Alex's office once more. "What do you think about making twelve hundred dollars a month? It sure beats walking around that complex."

I fumbled the words in my mouth several times. The law firm offering this salary was a prestigious one. They were going to give me $1,200 to work eight hours a day and have a lunch break, an hour lunch break. I was just awed.

The law firm was one of the largest in the city, with litigation, corporate, tax, and bankruptcy divisions. They had dozens of big bank, city, business, and industry clients.

"Listen, Jerrold, do you have any dress clothes?" Alex said. "You have to be dressed well in the business world. . . . We'll meet this weekend and get you some shoes and attire. You think about what you like and where you want to shop in the meantime. Also, there is something I want to tell you about where you'll be working. It's a very large, prestigious firm. Now most of these people probably have not had much contact with black people and couldn't tell you where south Dallas is. You don't have any education or office experience. Most of them are highly educated, experienced adults. You're going to have a lot of odds against you. They think that all black men are dumb, lazy criminals. You're going to have to go in there and prove yourself."

Listening to him really challenged me. These people didn't know anything about me and already had figured how and what I would be. They were the cream of the crop, the highly educated. And I was just a poor, ignorant, uneducated black boy from south Dallas. I would prove them all wrong.

I had been scheduled to start work the next month, so I decided to move back with my mother. This meant moving back to a tough part of south Dallas, but it was closer to downtown and on a better bus line. My mother was all excited about her son going to work for a law firm. And I myself had never been happier; persistence had paid off. Back home I went through south Dallas, telling my friends, Jamie, Vernon, his uncles, the old heads, my friends in Prince Hall, and everybody I could find. At home I would just stand in the mirror in my new shirt and jacket, feeling like a million dollars. "Man, you're lucky," my friends would say. They all wished they were in my shoes.

But Vernon felt disturbed about the whole thing. "Don't trust that white man too much. Don't get too close to him. He's one of those white men who realizes how wrong they are. He's just guilty now. He'll turn on you when you need him the most. He'll never be there through thick and thin."

I told Vernon I didn't have time for all that mess. Alex was asking for nothing in return; what could I have given him? What could he possibly want from me? No, I would trust him. He had been straightforward with me. He had been excited for me. I didn't care if he was white. He had enough compassion to see that there was no lack of talent, ambition, and will, but that I, no one, would ever get anywhere, get anything, without significant resources, some money, a start, some help.

And where were the black men? The ones who could have helped, the so-called middle class, the educated, the doctors, the professors, the businessmen, the politicians, the teachers, the entertainers, the sports figures? They had left us, got out of the slums and turned into Uncle Toms, puppets, and wanna-bes. Pretending they were so concerned with charity and giving back to the community, up there speculating on what they thought was the problem, refusing to have direct contact with us. Big fakers. I didn't understand why they couldn't stick together as a race. Meanwhile everyone was starving, struggling, and trying their damnedest to stay sane.

"Jerrold, you can think what you want, but I'm telling you, don't trust him. It won't last."

We just dropped the conversation after that, neither of us wanting to relent our position. Alex was here; and I didn't care what he, or his people, had done in the past. He had recognized a financial need and had offered to become my corporate mentor. I felt like his help was all I needed.

16

REBIRTH

One night in October 1989, as I lay in bed waiting to fall asleep for work the next morning, I heard a sudden, frantic knock on the front door. My mother, who was sleeping in the living room, and her boyfriend jumped up to see who was knocking. But I rushed past them, just in case some person with revenge on his mind was out there.

"Who is it?" I asked.

"It's Jonathan."

I told my mother to go back to bed, that it was only Vernon's brother.

I stood on the porch and shut the door. "What's the problem, man?" I asked.

He was frantic. "Aw, man, I tried to tell him to come on, but he just wouldn't listen."

Who was he talking about? I was in Jonathan's face now. "What the hell is wrong, man?"

His silent tears were dripping to the ground. "It's Vernon. He just got shot in the head."

Not Vernon, not my friend. He hadn't had his chance yet. He hadn't even begun to live. Jonathan was talking rapidly now.

"It was a dope dealer in Grand Prairie. Vernon whooped him in a fair fistfight. When we got ready to . . . to leave," he faltered, "the punk waited till we were far off, and fired his forty-five down at us. Vernon just turned, and looked at him, just stood there. Then he fell to the ground. He had a big hole in his jaw. The blood was gushing out like water. I tried to stop it."

Jonathan and I stood there in silence before I could ask him what I needed to know. "Is he dead?"

Jonathan relaxed. "I don't know, man. The ambulance took him to the hospital. He didn't look like he was breathing when they left. They were taking their time, not even attending to him."

He continued, "I told one of them to turn him on his back. I told him, 'Can't you see he can't breathe? He's drowning off his own blood.' The man looked up at me, then he slowly did it, and Vernon coughed and started back breathing."

I told Jonathan to go on home and I would be over later. I went inside and explained everything to my concerned mother. Then I called Vernon's grandmother. She said Vernon was alive, but in critical condition.

"He's going to live. There's nothing anyone can do right now. Just come by tomorrow, Jerrold," she said.

I was back in bed, but I wouldn't sleep. It was the last news I wanted to hear. I already had enough problems. After the first few months, things weren't going as well as I thought they would at work.

Oh, everything had started out fine: I had slid right into the middle of things with my first boss, a paralegal for one of the partners.

When we first met, she had taken me on a tour of all the different courts downtown, where later I would file papers for the lawyers. Walking back to the office from the tour on the second day I had known this woman, she had told me one of her secrets.

"My father hates blacks. I don't know why. He's been like that since I've known him. I mean, I don't see what's wrong with y'all or anything," she had said in her capricious fashion. She, like every person I would meet up there, seemed to have a million assumptions about blacks, things she wanted to explore.

In the beginning, my supervisor loved my performance. "You're so intelligent," she said. "I never imagined that."

I had been there for only a few months but had gotten the attention of a lot of people. The offices were all security coded, and on the hire date, management would assign the new employee his code. When I received mine, I looked at the piece of paper once, memorized the four-digit code, and threw it in the wastebasket.

"You must have a good memory," the hiring manager said.

I started off just running errands and copying documents. Yet the way I did that even surprised them. The courts were about three city blocks away. In the beginning someone said I was taking too long on trips, so I began to run full speed down to the court and back.

"How'd you get back here that fast? You must've zoomed down here," I'd hear.

Accuracy and speed were essential at the firm, for any small error could disrupt a case. I would work side by side with some of the best paralegals in the firm, scanning documents for witness files, putting documents in date order, and finishing two piles to their one. I wondered how some of them got any work done. They took so many breaks and "lady" conferences—while the clients were charged for hours of gossip.

If you need an assignment done fast, call Jerrold. If you have sixty boxes of documents and you need someone to skip lunch and work late on them, call Jerrold. "Jerrold, we can see you're way above average intelligence. The firm needs young, sharp people like yourself," said one of the supervisors.

"I heard how hard you worked on that case. Keep up the good work, Jerrold," said a partner.

I stayed mostly to myself, in my office with my piles of documents. To most of them, going through the thousands of pages of correspondence, memos, reports, and briefs, was dull work. To summarize a deposition made some of them pull their hair out. But I was like a kid in a candy factory. "He likes to write," they often said.

After work, on Tuesdays and Thursdays, I would sit for hours and read the correspondence from these big businesses, the engineers, chief officers, and bankers. I would take apart maybe two or three thousand pieces of paper, knowing I would have to put all that paper back in order. I would sit there and read these high-tech word battles, over and over. With this, I got a general sense of how industry works and a firsthand education in business writing.

When I wasn't reading the documents, I was in the law library, reading the case laws, the torts, all the books. I read everything that came across my desk. On Mondays, Wednesdays, and Fridays, I was at the community college, taking two classes, English and computer science, which were both a cinch. Everyone I knew back home could have performed highly. At night around nine, I would catch the bus home.

Before long, some of the attorneys were assigning work directly to me rather than going through the chain of command. They were so busy and under such pressure, they had time to worry only about who could get the job done quickly. One attorney even had me sit in a deposition with him for hours, to advise him on his questioning. As the paralegals saw and heard this, their mouths dropped open, their opinions changed.

Around then, too, a former clerk returned to the firm. I kept on working the same way, but no matter what I did after that, it was never right. If I had to work past lunch for an attorney, I was reprimanded for not taking lunch at noon. When an attorney would send for me, this clerk would, somehow, get the message before I did. I was shifted around to different paralegals.

I was finally assigned to the woman I surprised when she heard I could talk straight. I found her to be the least skilled of them all. She would make me look over her correspondence and reports to correct the mistakes. Once, I was going through about fifteen boxes of documents and saw a mistake that could have cost the law firm time and money. "You wasn't told to look for that," she screamed at me one day. People close by looked up.

A week later we were both called into the office meeting of one of the administrators.

"Jerrold, I understand there are problems with your speed. You're too slow."

I was so angry. I couldn't even find words. They were looking as if I were too dumb to comprehend what was going on. My supervisor added, "He found mistakes in the bates numbers. Perhaps he wants to go back through all the boxes."

"Yes, ma'am, I do," I said submissively, and heard, "Stop being so aggressive."

Some of the lower-level employees, like those in mail delivery, and also another case clerk, a Hispanic you would never guess was Hispanic, began to tell me in hushed tones that they had it in for me.

Then daily, slowly, all my morale left. Even though it seemed so untrue, I began to question myself. Maybe I had been doing everything wrong and it only looked right to me. Maybe they can see something that I just don't have the capacity to see. Maybe something in my head would not let me work the numbers right, could not let me think right, and everything was coming out backward.

In October I began to miss school to try to work harder, but it still was backward. No matter what I did, no matter how many times I looked over something, I couldn't satisfy these women. Then, over the next few months, my whole world began to crumble, I began having migraines and sleepless nights. I stopped eating, lost twenty-five pounds, and became skin and bones. I would sit in that office all day with my head pounding, just waiting to leave work. The whites seemed to sense this weakness, draw strength from it. I would leave work and curse the heavens for making me inferior. I was terrified to know that for the rest of my life, regardless of my determination, the only way I was going to get established was through the help of those white people, who would make my life miserable.

I couldn't read anymore, concentration was so hard to keep. I would just walk around the neighborhood, go shoot pool, or just drink with the fellows on the corner. I no longer wanted to work for that law firm, no longer wanted to be among white people. If I had to spend my life being miserable, it was going to be right here with the brothers, where at least, sometimes, I could get some relief.

I was experiencing the same impasse that had afflicted every black one of us, the same dilemma that crippled my mother, the dope dealers back in west Dallas, the man who made me steal the TV, sweet Gloria, Shortleg Lee, Syrup Head, Three Finger Willie, Drunk Tom, the old heads, the Dixon Circle dope dealers, and the workers—and especially my aunt's husband, who told me I would only get as far as the white man let me. He was right.

He was right because none of us had ever had any proof to the contrary. How can a man reason without knowledge? Where was our knowledge, our evidence? No one had ever told me I was capable of being a genius, building a city, pioneering new medicine, becoming an engineer. And if so, how would he have known? How would he have proven this to me, convinced a nineteen-year-old black boy that what had been reinforced all his life—through guileful TV, warped religion and education, through government propaganda and deception, Uncle Toms, and the so-called black leaders up there spitting out a lot of nonsense—was just a delusion? How could he disprove that the success of every black person was not somehow, always, tied into someone white: white teachers, white schools, white mentors, white history, white founding fathers? How could he explain that success was conceivable without white people? The evidence surely pointed to this. And, like everyone else I knew who was black, poor, and human, this is what I accepted.

The next morning I handled another day at the office, then prepared to see Vernon after work. On the way out, I felt as if I were leaving one white nightmare and entering another, the white walls, uniforms, and bedding of the hospital, a place that always gave me the creeps. The busy information center at Methodist directed me to intensive care. A family, grieving aloud, walked by. Their sorrow made me wonder if Vernon would look bad.

Once there, I stood outside his door, gathering enough courage to go inside. From the hall I saw two doctors taking pictures of his face.

I walked in and bent near him. The blackish swelling made his face and neck look like old, limp balloons. The doctors must have noticed the same breathing problem that had upset Jonathan because they had cut a large hole in his throat. A thick tube attached to a machine bloated in the hole. He held his mouth wide open and sucked air in slowly. I realized that Vernon was going to be laid up for a while. I gripped my compassionate friend's hand as he continued to rest.

Several days later the doctors gave a positive prognosis. He had no brain or spinal injuries, maybe some nerve damage. During the next three months he remained in the hospital, where he underwent reconstructive operations. He was so charismatic that the surgeons decided to treat him for free.

Afterward I went to visit him several times. He was usually heavily sedated, so I never stayed long. His body was strong, and he was recovering faster than normal. After he was released, he moved in with his mother.

*   *   *

Back at the duplex, my mother had driven her latest boyfriend away. Now, since he was gone, she mostly stayed away from the house, so I saw her less frequently, maybe three times a week. But one week, she stayed away for many days. During what I thought would be a normal evening, I came home from work to another empty house. The heroin had again made her sell everything that we owned. At times like this, when something was pushing her to the edge of insanity, she had no mercy. She did whatever it took to hold on. She even sold my work clothes and school books. More important, though, she sold the dresser in which I kept the receipts for the money I sent to Vanessa. This meant I wouldn't be able to prove I had taken care of her. I sat on the porch all that night, meditating on the situation, trying to figure out a plan. Although I only had the clothes on my back, I was so hardened that her actions no longer affected me.

I called Vernon for help. He convinced his mother to let me move in with them. The few weeks that I stayed there, I stayed close to him. His mother let us have the upstairs room, which had a giant closet that we converted into a room, adding a bed, a TV, and a phone. Vernon now weighed about 135 pounds. His tongue had been sewn to his mouth, and his mouth was wired shut. He could only drink liquids and eat very soft foods. He smoked weed a lot, because of the pain, which had increased after each of the several surgeries he'd had. In that room I stayed with him, listening to music or talking for hours. And with my paychecks, I bought him medicine, weed, special foods, and anything else he requested.

I later moved in with my sister for two months. She still lived in the apartments in Pleasant Grove. With the money I saved while living there, I rented a small, cozy apartment on Ferguson Road. The apartments were in east Dallas, on the fast 64 Ferguson bus route, which meant I would have no problem getting to and from work.

Over the past months, I had continued to meet with Alex,

even though he now made me feel uncomfortable. Lately I was feeling the same kind of distrust of him. I knew without a doubt that Alex would never love me like my own people, would never go all the way for me, like Vernon, especially if it meant confronting his own people. And some of his remarks shook me up.

On the day I moved into my new apartment, he came and helped. That day I asked Alex why he was continuing to assist me. He stopped and looked hard at me. He said, "Well, it's better than us coming down here with rifles and shooting a bunch of y'all up."

He was serious. I wondered, as I looked at him, who was the "us" he was talking about? Was he describing a bunch of white people storming black neighborhoods with guns? I was confused by his comments because Alex wasn't some Klan member or skinhead. Alex was a respected member of his community who taught little white kids in Sunday school each week. He was a man with strong influence.

Also, I remembered when he visited my house in south Dallas, after I joined the firm. It was a day when automatic gunfire exploded in the near distance. When he heard the shots, Alex took one look at me and scrambled to get inside his BMW. Guns and death clearly terrified him.

In addition, Alex had been inquiring about my activities at the firm as though he were a dedicated scientist conducting an experiment, always dead serious. I felt obligated to answer his questions since he had found the job for me, but it made me uneasy. And during one of his inquiries, a paralegal told him I was on probation. When he mentioned it to me, I told him I thought that the whites there were being very unfair with me, and that I was thinking about resigning. Alex said not to worry about it, that he had figured the job would be too tough for somebody like me.

I continued going to work, even though I had just about given up. At the new apartment in Pleasant Grove, I spent my time just sitting around or staying up all night. Sometimes I caught the bus over to Vernon's to keep him company. He was encouraging me to keep the job, to hold on as long as I could.

I tried to visit my little girl as often as possible, but that meant putting up with Tammie. She was now an eighteen-year-old who wanted to ponder the secrets of men, clubs, parties, and excitement. Several friends had told me that Tammie was going with a dope dealer. She later admitted that she had allowed one to have a private phone installed in her house, so she could make phone calls for him and receive his messages. As a consequence of Tammie's activities, Vanessa was mostly left with Tammie's grandmother, who ensured her good health.

As another consequence, I didn't see Vanessa too often—only when Tammie was in a good mood or didn't have male company, or when I would bring money or gifts over. But my determination to love and support Vanessa would remain intact, even though I often left there more miserable than when I arrived, because of Tammie.

On one of these lost evenings, when I was at the lowest stage of my life, when I had nobody to instill confidence in me with proof and not the empty statements I had heard all my life, I sat at my apartment. I had the window in my small bedroom open, and the hot night air was blowing through. Even though it wasn't that hot and I had taken off my shirt, I was still sweating in my small bed as I lay there. There was no future for me at this point. Some of my essays and poems, which I kept in a box, were scattered on the room floor. So were my once revered dress clothes. I sifted through some of the writing, reminiscing on old times. I was sweating so hard that the sweat was dripping on the papers. Heat had always come at a time of crisis in my life.

From childhood, I had been a curious person, had bugged everyone I thought had an answer or a clue, and later had delved into books to gain understanding. But nothing could answer why I felt like something was internally wrong, why black life was a paradox. The reality before me, as it was, showed in all its aspects that I and everybody I knew were limited individuals, innate failures, black nobodies. I understood then how people became dope dealers, how women and men could abandon their children, their race, pride, manhood, and womanhood. It was clear now, easy to see why blacks had become parasites on each other.

I still kept my boxes of books with me. Reading was second nature by now. So I turned to the only escape I had ever known, which could easily have been drugs but, for me, was books. I picked up the one Fahim had given me, the weathered book with the black man on the cover. It was the *Autobiography of Malcolm X*, written with the assistance of Alex Haley. Though it was painstaking reading at first, I kept at it all evening and into the night. At last! Here was one, an example, though dead. A black man who was purely himself. I was so overwhelmed, I stayed up the entire night pondering the black hero. Malcolm said get off your knees and fight your own battle. That's the way to win back your self-respect. That's the way to make the white man respect you. And if he won't let you live like a man, he certainly can't keep you from dying like one!

The next day I shared the book with Vernon. It had the same effect, simply overwhelmed him.

After reading about Malcolm's life, I realized something. I couldn't recall one strong black man in my youth. This had been pervasive in every situation. Most of the women were husbandless, all the children fatherless. Where were the black soothing hands in our moments of uncertainty? Where was the black man's wisdom and guidance to lead us around snares and guide us through tribulation? Where was my father, who resists despair and holds high his torch of hope?

Malcolm's life story was the first confirmation I was looking for in my quest for understanding. I began to search more than I ever had before, reading more than I had at the West Dallas Public Library.

From that little apartment, I lived like a hermit for about two months, only going out for work or for food. Inside, I would sit in the living room or across my bed, reading about all the dead black heroes, philosophers, and thinkers. I learned about people like Marcus Garvey, who attempted to unite all the black people of the world; Professors Cheikh Anta Diop and Ivan Van Sertima and their extraordinary research in documenting our accomplishments; McCoy, an inventor whose products were so good that everyone wanted "the real McCoy"; Garret Morgan, who invented the gas mask and traffic light; Jan Matzeliger, who invented the first shoe-making machine (lathe) and revolutionized that industry; and hundreds more. What impressed me most is that they never relinquished their right to equal respect as humans.

More important, I learned about people like Imhotep the Great, the world's first multigenius, who lived around 2970 B.C. Imhotep was considered the father of modern medicine, and he built the world's first hospital, called the Temple of Hotep. He was a great architect and designed the Step Pyramid. Imhotep was revered as one of the wisest men in the world. He's responsible for the famous phrase "Eat, drink, and be merry, for tomorrow you die."

And there were black women like Queen Kahina, a woman who rallied forces and fought fiercely against Arabs who invaded and conquered parts of Africa, such as Egypt, a place they still occupy. Did you know that Greeks learned at the feet of African men? The philosophies they took back to Greece were foreign in their own country, and they were often persecuted for introducing such beliefs.

I learned that the Egyptians had the world's greatest university, the mystery schools, where it took students fifty years to become masters. In the beginning only Egyptians could study there, but later they also accepted Greeks and Persians, whom they called babies in knowledge. The Egyptians called themselves the Kemets, which means black people. Their education consisted of the ten virtues and the seven liberal arts. Grammar, rhetoric, logic, arithmetic, and geometry were studied. And at the highest levels they taught the supersciences.

All my life I had said "Amen" at the end of prayers, never

knowing that it was a word blacks used before the Bible was written, to give homage to life. Here was the true laying down of the foundation of all knowledge. My founding fathers.

Why wasn't I told that we came to America before Columbus, carrying gold-tipped spears; or that we were being taught what we once had taught others? Why wasn't I told that Africa was here when Europe didn't exist? Or that the subjects of the original *Madonna and Child* had been black and the work later resculptured to bear the image of white people, and that paintings and icons of the son of God had been done over for the same purpose? No wonder everyone had felt naturally disturbed at the little west Dallas church.

My discovery of dead literary role models permanently cured my doubt and made me bind back to the fundamental truth. Knowing the great accomplishments of my people, when they existed in their own civilizations, started a chain reaction that would change the foundation of my mind. But this change had nothing to do with my drive and confidence. These had always been there. Deep inside every person I had met, where it has retreated to its last, safe sanctuary, the spirit lived.

Just as I realized it had with me, the potential of most people I had known, while starving in the west Dallas housing projects, while wandering in Oak Cliff, while decaying in Prince Hall, had been subdued by this defect in understanding. Vernon, Jamie, Shelvin . . . The greatest loss to all of us was not the loss of our parents, our families, and our education, not the disappointment, the hunger, and the humiliation. It was the loss of our minds, for the mind is the soul of man.

After learning the buried truth, that we were the first, the fathers of knowledge, the unhomed children of the sun, I felt that my entire life had been like that of a certain man who had wings of strength and splendor. From childhood this man had watched his brethren sweep the heavens and glide gracefully in the sunshine. But because his wings were a different color, he had been fooled into believing he could not fly. He knew his wings looked the same, were built the same, flapped the same. But he never had proof. So he never had tried. Then he discovered in a remote cave, a cave that had been kept well hidden, pictures of men of his color, flying in the clouds. And on this glorious day, in desperation, he jumped off a cliff, was swooped up in the winds of truth, flapped his damnedest, and found he could fly above them all.

17

OUT OF THE MADNESS

Full of new assurance, I eventually returned to my original performance level at the firm. While still there, I worked feverishly, coordinating several projects at a time, seeking out paralegals to get assignments, and doing clutch work for several attorneys. I was there to see the cleaning crews leave at nights.

And instead of being docile and content, I became outspoken. I would challenge the whites on the spot whenever they tried to use their inferiority tactics. I began, for example, to keep time schedules, notes, and dates, and whenever they would make up a lie about my speed or proficiency, I would whip out those charts and dates and watch them turn red.

Eventually, I was fired because "we just can't seem to place confidence in you," said one. "People are uncomfortable. Maybe it's better," said another. However, until I was released, I worked my hardest to break every stereotype they had.

On my last day there in late March 1990, I told them all it had been a pleasure working with them. I calmly walked around the office and shook the hands of several people I had come to know. I heard later that some attorneys protested my departure. But I was more than ready to get away from there, a place I felt had only limited me.

I called Alex to let him know I had been fired. He said, "Maybe you just weren't ready."

I asked him if he wanted to hear my side of the story. He told me, "It doesn't matter. I'm still your friend. I believe in you."

I wanted Alex to admit it was possible for those whites to be unfair, but this was something I don't think he could do. I would call Alex periodically for the next few weeks, to see if he wanted to talk. I still liked him and thought we could be friends on a different level, without him trying to help me, just plain old friends. But he wouldn't return my calls. I finally figured he had given up hope and was trying to let me off easy. So I stopped calling.

Although Alex and I needed time away from each other, we would eventually talk and grow close again, especially after my reputation as a rising writer began to build in the South. I knew he had felt that no matter how strong and motivated I was, my task was hopeless. And his presence had represented a life that I could not have. But I knew otherwise.

Knowing harder times were on the horizon, I had paid my rent up for two months. And I had a few hundred dollars of severance pay. But I ended up giving that money to a friend who was behind on his rent, all except enough to buy a desk, several textbooks, and a small file cabinet.

With my apartment as a base, I began to sort out a life plan. Even though I should have been worried, even though I knew my money would run out soon and that I would be back in the middle of the lowest levels of poverty, worry was the farthest thing from my mind. My findings had stirred something deep in me. And now only time kept me from learning.

I felt I also could invent mathematical formulas to build architecture like the Pyramids, whose formulas still baffle all of science. If my people had invented surgical instruments and were performing brain surgery when other countries were in the Dark Ages, if my people had complex forms of governments and systems of religions when other races were primitive, then I could also accomplish high tasks. If my people knew of the rings of Saturn, the moons of Jupiter, and the interpretations of the stars before there were telescopes, then these mental aptitudes were also available to me. The same core for this intelligence, this mass understanding, this interpretation of complexity, flowed in my veins. And I intended to use every drop of it or die trying.

I would begin each morning at my desk, after a small breakfast, working on strategy and goals. I knew I had no intention of doing a step-by-step struggle to the top of the success ladder, going through years of toiling with the white business community and its owners so I could say, "Gee, after twenty years, I am a successful store manager working eighty hours a week, making pennies and crumbs." I no longer had the patience for the politics and racism at some rigid white company. So I figured I would work on projects and ideas that could catapult me over that stage, through those unnecessary setbacks, and into an area where I had some real financial independence.

This was nothing new. Many of the young men had come to the same conclusion, that enough of us had been taught to have small dreams, to say "I want to be a doctor," rather than "I want to own a hospital," to say "I want to be a manager," rather than "I want to own and control a large industry," to say "I want to be a teacher," rather than "I want to pioneer a new university," or write math and history books, or design new computers, and build houses, and similar dreams. But I realized we were doing in decades what it had taken other races centuries to do, and against odds a hundred times greater.

I concluded that my first objective must be to gain a base of understanding on as many subjects as I could. I realized that learning new disciplines, such as trigonometry, law, agriculture, nuclear science, was a core thing, meaning any person can shape his intelligence to master any body of knowledge he desires. So I began with writing and decided math would be next. I always had figured it's better to master one discipine before moving on to another. So that's the way I studied, mostly the art of writing, and occasionally studying math, business, and other areas. I figured once I had mastered writing, I would move on to math, then decide what would be next.

Over time, I began to read the textbooks I had bought. I started from the very beginning, reading grammar, essay, and rhetoric books. I knew I had to patch up the holes in my knowledge, everything I had missed in grade school. Instead of just reading, I would memorize the information, thirty and forty pages of text, word for word, and practice quoting the text verbatim. I had always heard the remark "You have to be twice as good as the white man to make it." And now I understood. I inevitably would do the same with the math, memorizing the rules and steps, the formulas. I would do the same with vocabulary, typing, basic computer programming, and dozens of other subjects.

I no longer thought of just being a writer, scientist, or attorney, which were my first ambitions. Why not all? My confidence was that high. I knew it was possible and less difficult than I had been led to believe. Besides, so many of us had been killed, imprisoned, or warped that we needed men and women who had more than one skill, in order to rebuild our communities.

The only difference between us and others is that they had all the resources: food, books, air conditioners, parents, organized communities, banks, schools, newspapers, grocery stores, a right to a fair trial, a right to decent medical care, protection from police officers, fair opportunity, taxation with representation, and other important things. Furthermore, we were facing a wide information gap, because we once weren't allowed even to read and learn. And when that was abolished we were given inferior schools, misinformation, and terrorized neighborhoods. And the gap between the races became wider and wider. As a result, I knew, and took pride in knowing, that the status of white America, all their gains, wasn't something that they had earned through fair competition. They couldn't stand proudly and say, "We earned, and worked, and toiled for this. Y'all had equal opportunity, y'all are just dumb and lazy." Whites had never competed fairly for anything. No one truly knew the measure of their ability. Instead, they had killed off and enslaved others for the wealth and resources they possessed and had held on to at any price.

After a while, after I felt I had really started to change my direction, I finally went back to south Dallas to find my friends. I ran into Jamie first, near Lincoln High School. He was happy to see me. "Where have you been, Jelly Roll?" he asked, using the nickname he had given me. He was coming from Lincoln where he now worked as a teacher's assistant.

He took me to a small white house on Pine Street that he was renting, which was several blocks from the school. I told Jamie I would be needing a place to stay. Without hesitation, he asked if I wanted to move in. "You know you're welcome to live with me," he said.

So a few days later, I paid one of the older men in south Dallas to haul my belongings to his house. Jamie gave me one of the two bedrooms, the one in the back. And to help him with the bills, I filed for unemployment.

Back in the neighborhood, I settled into my new home, my new back room, with my small desk and boxes of books, and went right back to work. I enrolled into two summer classes at the community college and started looking for a part-time job. I still stayed mostly in the house, except for occasionally going out with Jamie and his friends.

I began to work on the first rough drafts of my life story and other small writings that would be published in magazines in Texas. I later would win several prestigious writing awards and be invited to visit Ethel Kennedy in her house in McLean, Virginia, where I met Senator Ted Kennedy, who encouraged me to keep up the good work. I eventually would use my writing talents to pave the way for me to pursue my entrepreneurial ambitions.

I saw little of Vernon during this time but learned he had begun selling dope in Arlington, a suburb about twenty minutes from Dallas. He was getting into lots of fights and staying around trouble. He even tried to start fights with Jamie and me. So we figured he would have to find himself in his own time, believed he would choose the right path before it was too late, but decided, for the time being, to support him from a distance.

By the summer of my twentieth birthday, I had learned the truth about self-reliance, about not wasting my intellect, about my responsibility to my child. I had not thrown away courage, become a dope addict or a religious puppet. But I still saw my friends shooting each other, saw the girls walking the streets like zombies, saw the hardworking Dixon Circle boys losing hope.

I was keenly aware of where I stood, that there was no real racial harmony or freedom for blacks, and anyone who claimed so was a fool. I knew I had no time to waste, that there was too much that needed changing and too much work to get done.

So I committed myself to being a living testimony, to being a custodian of black proverbs and lore, to writing great race-guiding books, ones that would encourage us once again to explore, to value family, culture, and unity.

It was at this time, in the heart of a bitter neighborhood called south Dallas, in a place where the suffering of the people has no bounds, that I knew I had won the fight for my soul. With this victory, I realized that nothing, and no one, could ever stop me from living and dying as a strong black man, that I was forever out.

EPILOGUE

In the summer of 1992, while living with my sister in Oak Cliff near Paul Quinn College, I met a new friend: Keenon, a young man about twenty years old. We talked about his motorcycle's horsepower at a black-owned detail shop on Lancaster Street, Sparkle Detail, one street over from where old man Wayne had lived.

Keenon was about my height (six feet one), had real dark skin, and permed shoulder-length hair, which was popular with black men in 1992. We both had slim builds, but I was larger from lifting weights, and he was gangly. After we talked, he burned rubber as he left the detail shop, his hair fluttering in the breeze. He leaned around a corner and out of sight. He was gone so quickly.

Over the two months I knew him, we did many things together. We rode around in my convertible Mustang. He tried to teach me to ride his fast bike—I backed out after I saw him run into a fence with that thing. We ate pizza at his grandmother's house, where his only brother lived and his mother, stepfather, and younger sister, who had a small child, visited all the time.

Over time, I learned Keenon had qualities I admired: quiet, understanding, observant, and extra-kindhearted—a kindness some mistook for weakness. And Keenon, similar to most of the hardened brothers, was not afraid to exchange blows with any man, although that wasn't his preference.

Keenon had one of the best personalities. He had a charming smile, which was full, pearly and deep. Being around him, you knew that there wasn't anything he wouldn't do for you—if he loved you. Keenon's mother had lost her job, so he had taken up a lot of the slack. He told me he'd been paying many of the bills at the apartment where they lived, including, at times, the five-hundred-dollar rent. He also helped his sister and his grandmother. All of his family looked up to him.

But I never imagined Keenon sold drugs to get the money. He seemed too smart to slip into that trap. One day while we talked in front of his house, he asked for a ride to some nearby apartments.

"For what?" I asked.

"To pick up some dope," he said, smiling a little. "I'll just run up there and be right back down."

But he stopped smiling when he saw how amazed I was. He started looking amazed, too, as if he couldn't believe I was surprised over something so common, something everybody was doing for a little change. I refused to take him.

About two weeks later, Keenon rode with me near Red Bird Mall to pick up the keys to my new apartment. Going there, I told him how I felt about him taking chances selling drugs, how I felt he should put his intellect to better use. "I'm about to incorporate a small company," I told him.

During that trip home, he must have asked a thousand questions about the goals of this company and how was I doing it.

He sadly reminded me of many former close friends, and other people I had known who desired to establish legitimate means of income, to own companies, to chart their own destinies. But, just like the challenges they faced, Keenon would need strength to overcome the difficulties of his life.

Keenon would never have the chance to grow into the man he could have become, never have the chance to reflect on his glorious past or tap the greatness sleeping within him. The last time I saw him alive was when he and his stepfather helped me move my belongings into my new apartment. Days later, I came over while his stepfather stood outside the house of Keenon's grandmother. "Hey, where's Keenon?" I asked.

"Jerrold, Keenon's dead," he said. "He spent the night here, and when we came this morning, we found him, his brother, his grandmother, and his friend piled up on the floor. They were all dead, had been shot execution-style. The whole kitchen floor was soaked in blood."

For the next two weeks, people in cars would slowly pass the house to see where the murders had occurred. It was reported as one of the most gruesome mass killings in Dallas. It kept the black neighborhoods paralyzed for a long time. The Dallas media played Keenon up like some sort of big drug lord, which upset his family.

A young man in his mid-twenties was caught and convicted nearly a year later for all four murders. He was allegedly a drug rival of Keenon's.

Keenon's death had so much significance. Another friend gone. Another senseless murder.

Keenon was just another black boy destroyed, proving that the factory of death was still churning, and that the black race must work hard to solve the dilemma of the mind.

Around then, I helped my mother and her elder husband move to my two-bedroom apartment. She had lived down the street from Keenon's grandmother and had seen him hanging in her apartment complex. Keenon had kept the young boys from disrespecting her when she entered and left her house. I encouraged her to pack her bags and move several days later.

She had been on and off drugs the last two years, and in and out of jail. I had left for Florida in December 1991 to attend Florida A&M, and had returned home in April 1992. She had gone to jail the same week I returned home. It took a lot of time, effort, and money to gain her release. While I was in Florida, she had found a man she admired and gotten married. She was now forty-two. We moved in together to the new apartment, where she finally was in a position with some real support.

She enrolled in GED classes on her own, and got more involved with her grandchildren. She talked to me about her desire to develop a program to treat addicts and people in need. She felt that she knew how to counsel and respect those kinds of individuals and wanted to do her part in contributing to improving our community. I promised her that as long as she had dreams like that I would make sure she had all the support she needed. It would fulfill another goal of mine: to design a family treatment facility around her theories.

I had heard my mother many times tell me never to let God get fed up and turn his back on you. "Once he does this, you're no longer under his protection," she had warned. I guess her friend Big Mary never learned this lesson. One day she fell dead in a Dallas street. Others we knew fared better. Shortleg Lee is still alive, retired, and living in south Dallas. I've had little contact with Vernon. Jamie got married and does his own audio and visual production work.

My sister remains married, and has added a son to her posse— my nieces, Fatima and Shakara. Her marriage is really working and she is settled and happy. She also plans to return to school. My brother has a daughter and a son by an older woman he lives with. He is enrolled in the police training course at Dallas Baptist University and plans to become a police officer. We all guess that's okay for three high school dropouts.

Vanessa knows her daddy, and we are finally getting the chance to do all the things that a father and daughter should do. There's so much I've gone through with her mother in trying to be a responsible father. I missed the first two years of Vanessa's life dealing with Tammie. The court recognized me as Vanessa's father and I've been given visitation rights. It was pure torture getting Vanessa adjusted. Even to this day, I feel that Tammie's keeping Vanessa away from me and making things difficult was the most undeserved thing that ever happened to me. In the present, Tammie remains uncooperative about the whole arrangement. But Vanessa and I don't worry about that.

After returning from Florida A&M University—the school would only support my education if I majored in journalism—I reenrolled at a community college here in Dallas, planning to someday major in psychology and economics at an area university. I have incorporated a small company, to produce quality film, music, and literature for African Americans, and I intend to develop a finance company in the near future, to develop business and industry in the black communities. And I'll continue writing.

I regret so much that I was unable to offer my friend Keenon an alternative. None of us can give him his flowers now. But I hope we can one day give redemption to all of our young black men and women who have died without ever living. This redemption will come only when we tear down the factory of destruction that produces the mass death of our young.

I hope all the adversity I have suffered in life and what I have gained from this benefits you in some way. While writing this book, I opened my heart and died for you. So please do your part for us, however small it may be. We, the black race, need you to stay faithful and strong, and to never give up on us.

AFTERWORD
by
Fahim Minkah

At age forty-nine, I was just coming out of several years of rest, having been a freedom fighter all my life: I founded and chaired for several years the Texas State Chapter of the Black Panther Party based in Dallas. During my younger years I was a devout follower of Malcolm X, and a student of Mao Tse-tung, the leader of the Chinese revolution. I spent my life fighting for the freedom of oppressed people, and had spent several years in prison. After I entered my forties, I was forced into exile, a time when I concentrated on developing a business and supporting my family.

But in 1988 there were dangers on the horizon which threatened to eliminate the black race in America. It was then that I saw the absolute effect of drug dealers taking over neighborhoods, and then that I learned of the unprecedented potency of new drugs like crack cocaine. I was amazed at the new kind of inner city crime, the drive-by shootings, the gang activity, how these elements were chipping away at communities in Dallas we once had organized. As the father of seven children, I had no choice but to come from my exile and rejoin the battle.

It was around this time that I first met Jerrold Ladd, and I knew immediately there was something special about him. He and his friends attended a speech I was giving, and Jerrold stared at me the whole forty-five minutes without saying a word. He was really thin looking, but sturdy, and had a book in his hand. He also had a gleam in his eyes, the kind that illuminates greatness.

Over the next few years I would grow close to Jerrold, and come to know him and his unique ways very well; he eventually would regard me as the closest person to him.

Without a degree in anything, Jerrold has become the master of many things, all self-taught. His writing style is completely original. As a storyteller, he excels as a natural of the African guru fashion. He is able to describe characters in a way that leaves the reader feeling like you met them yourself.

From the many books we've exchanged I have witnessed his love for reading. He can read all day, and he won't let you disturb him either. I have seen him research and acquaint himself with technical subjects within hours. He has a passion for the law, and I wouldn't be surprised if one day he added a law degree to his résumé. I'm proud to say that this young black man is on a path to making a mark on America, not just as a writer, but in whatever else he chooses to engage in.

What can I say about *Out of the Madness*, except that it is a work of true greatness. In this, I do not view Jerrold as a "black writer," but as an up-and-coming contemporary American writer whose future holds great promise. And his book will teach us to love and cherish every drop of black blood in our bodies.

However, no one will benefit from these lessons if we continue to let ourselves become engulfed in bitterness, turn into thieves and dope dealers, and keep despising one another. There's nothing redeeming or glamorous about selling drugs, because this act is capable of destroying our entire race. So any attempt to sell or distribute drugs should be viewed as an act against the people, especially in places like the projects, and in other such communities where the enviroment has a marked destructive impact on black families, male and female alike.

But Jerrold says to us, your enviroment alone should not determine your destiny. No matter how dire the circumstances a person encounters, he or she can make correct choices, develop inner strength, and choose the right path. Look at Jerrold and his brother and sister, a family of kids who have, under some of the most trying and torturous circumstances, endured. This says that we all can.

Social scientists may be tempted to say that Jerrold "fell through the cracks" after reading about the environment of despair that he grew up in. But this is not so. Jerrold must be given all the credit for his deliberate struggle, for keeping his sanity, and excelling as he has done. Ultimately, he must also be praised for calling for the awakening of the black spirit. And she must answer.

ACKNOWLEDGMENTS

I sincerely wish to thank the following people for their part in my life.

The majestic power, God, who shall lead his flock out of bondage. My mother, Carol Morgan, the unhomed queen, whose true wisdom was never known, and whose imperishable kingdom was never found. My daughter, Vanessa Jacqua Ladd, who is a blessing to her father and made in my image. My brother and sister, William Paul Ladd, Jr., and Sherrie Lenette Greer, who also endured the fire.

My nieces and nephews, Fatima and Shakara Greer, Marcus Greer, Jr., Akeema Rena Ladd (Poo-Pahna), and William Paul Ladd the 3rd. Sherrie's husband, Marcus Greer. My extended family, especially my aunt Felisa Evans. God knows your hearts. I thank my grandmother on my father's side of the family, Frankie Ladd, who did try to help us once when we were small.

The black women who showed me kindness: Angela Norton, whose sweetness is a blessing to the world, Cassandra Hill and her mother, Mrs. Ialine Burch Hill, who took me into their house and loved me. Shontina Nicole Rachelle Mack, whose life was more horrible than mine, but who is a fine, determined young woman; Shontina will always be my special friend. Edwina Sullivan, Christina Samuels, Markesha Beal. And Vanessa Collins, who believed in me enough to type the first rough drafts of this book in 1990. You are so special.

Barron and Kevin Smith, Johnny Nutson, Michael and "Buddy" Carter; everybody I know from west and south Dallas, and Dixon Circle, where I lived in the four-bedroom; Elgin Glenn Young, who is an inspiring writer; and Ricky Dixon, a professional football player from Dallas.

I also thank Mr. Fahim Jabari Minkah (formerly Fred Bell), who is the most brilliant black leader in Texas. Bob Ray Sanders, who has been a special friend and mentor, and who gave me pointers throughout my work. Doug Owen. Charles R. O'Neal, the publisher of the *Dallas Examiner*, where I held my first reporting job. Charles has uncompromising love for his people and is the best editorial writer in America. Lawrence Young, Vernon Smith, Kevin Merida, Jason Johnson, Rochelle Riley, all black journalists of the *Dallas Morning News* who nurtured me one way or the other. Irwin Thompson, the brother who took the cover photo. Bob Mong, the managing editor of the *Dallas Morning News*, who has been my most consistent, reliable supporter. Bill Evans, executive managing editor at the *News*, who always smiled warmly at me. Chris Kelley, Brooks Egerton, and others at the *Dallas Morning News*. Mr. Joe Black. My attorney, Michael Sean Quinn, who has the most logical mind I know, and an expert litigator. And Vince Ackerson, my business partner.

My agent, David H. Smith, who believed in this book when no one else would. My editor, Mauro DiPreta, who has always treated me with special respect and good humor; I hope we can work together on every project I write. The staff at Warner Books, especially Susan Walker Moffat and Maureen Mahon Egen, who took me in and treated me like a superstar. (Boy that felt great!) I hope I make a good investment.

The doctors at Parkland Memorial Hospital in Dallas who fixed my hand at three in the morning and joked with me before surgery. (I told y'all.) My doctor, Jerel R. Biggers.

And everyone I failed to mention. I thank you all.